max science primary

Student Book 5

DISCOVERING THROUGH ENQUIRY

LAWRIE RYAN

SERIES EDITOR: BOB KIBBLE

macmillan education

INTERNATIONAL CURRICULUM

Macmillan Education
4 Crinan Street
London N1 9XW
A division of Springer Nature Limited

Companies and representatives throughout the world

Student Book ISBN 978-1-380-02167-0
Digital Student Pack ISBN 978-1-380-02434-3
Student Bundle Pack ISBN 978-1-380-02436-7

First published 2019

Original design by EMC Design Ltd and Macmillan Education
Page make-up by Tek-Art Ltd
Illustrated by Ilias Arahovitis pp 2, 8, 12, 13, 17, 28, 30, 31, 37, 40, 42, 43, 52, 56, 68, 70, 76, 78, 82, 90, 91, 98, 107, 114, 123, 127, 128, 133 c/o Beehive Illustration; Martin Cain pp 5, 11, 15, 16, 18, 20, 33, 35, 38, 41, 47, 53, 70, 71, 73, 75, 83, 84, 87, 92, 93, 105, 108, 113, 116, 117, 122, 131, 132, 143 c/o Beehive Illustration; Moreno Chiacchiera pp 3, 14, 19, 26, 32, 45, 50, 51, 53, 59, 61, 64, 66, 67, 68, 70, 71, 80, 88, 92, 100, 101, 110, 112, 118, 125, 128 c/o Beehive Illustration; Eric Smith pp 9, 23, 27, 29, 33, 77, 91, 95, 108, 111, 113, 119, 129 c/o Beehive Illustration

Cover design by Sparks Publishing Services Ltd and Macmillan Education
Cover illustration by Star Publishing Pte Ltd and Jorge Santillan c/o Beehive Illustration Agency
Picture research by Susannah Jayes

The author and publishers would like to thank the following for permission to reproduce their photographs:

Alamy/MIHAI ANDRITOIU p109, Alamy/Matthew Chattle p13, Alamy/Custom Life Science p42, Alamy/Ian G Dagnall p99(cr), Alamy/eye35stock p25(cr), Alamy/Tim Gainey p56(br), Alamy/Glasshouse Images p94, Alamy/Rob Gordon p24(bl), Alamy/Eliza Henderson p21(cmr), Alamy/Karl Kost p95, Alamy/National Geographic Images Collection p103(br), Alamy/Universal Images Group North America LLC/DeAgostini p40(cl), Alamy/Victorcity p130t, Alamy/John Wellings p95; **Data Harvest** p130(cr); **Getty Images** p63(cr), Getty Images/AlexandrBognat p27, Getty Images/amperesey p12(2), Getty Images/Stefanie Baum p79, Getty Images/Nigel Cattlin p85, Getty Images/cezars p43(tl), Getty Images/Peter Chadwick LRPS p73(c), Getty Images/CreativeNature_nl p72, Getty Images/Ekspansio p115(br), Getty Images/John Elk III p12(4), Getty Images/Encyclopedia Britannica/UIG p103(cl, bl), Getty Images/Martyn Goddard p126, Getty Images/Vladmir Godnik p6(tr), Getty Images/George Grall p62(bl), Getty Images/Tommy Hindley/Professional Sport/Popperfoto p7, Getty Images/Andrew Holt p26(cr), Getty Images/iStockphoto/Thinkstock/James Thew p2(br), Getty Images/iStockphoto/Thinkstock/Richard Whitacre p89, Getty Images/jrroman p6(cr), Getty Images/Brian E. Kushner p104(tr), Getty Images/Pat Law Photography pp2–3, Getty Images/Ch'ien Lee/Minden Pictures p63(cl), Getty Images/Sebastien Lemyre p57(br), Getty Images/The LIFE Images Collection p103(cr), Getty Images/mariusFM77 p9, Getty Images/Emilija Mavenska p10, Getty Images/minermero p6(br), Getty Images/Darlyne A. Murawski p62(tr), Getty Images/narvikk p115(bl), Getty Images/nightman1965 p90, Getty Images/Nikographer (Jon) p57(bl), Getty Images/Lisa Olson/EyeEm p110, Getty Images/Ignacio Palacios p43(tr), Getty Images/Chonlachai Panprommas/EyeEm p5, Getty Images/Kcris Ramos p12(1), Getty Images/Jose B. Ruiz/Nature Picture Library p24(br), Getty Images/RysersonClark p21(cr), Getty Images/Graham Sheehan/EyeEm p23, Getty Images/Prakash Singh p16, Getty Images/Southern Lightscapes-Australia p29, Getty Images/Squareman p49(bm), Getty Images/Stan Strange/EyeEm p48, Getty Images/Studio Omg/EyeEm p124, Getty Images/web20000ra p25(br), Getty Images/Peter Welke/EyeEm p55(t), Getty Images/Westend61 p6(tc); **Photodisc**/Getty Images p120(torch); **PNAS** March 6, 2012 109 (10) 4008-4013 https://doi.org/10.1073/pnas.1118386109 p75; **Rex Shutterstock**/Joe Castro/EPA-EFE p2(br); **Science Photo Library** p41(bcm); **Shutterstock**/2523studio p73(tr), Shutterstock/Africa Studio p34, Shutterstock/amophoto_au p21, Shutterstock/Aphelleon p89(bl), Shutterstock/Darren Baker p12(3), Shutterstock/Narubas Bangpasert p41, Shutterstock/Phil Darby p56(bmr), Shutterstock/Sebastian Duda p22, Shutterstock/fenkieandreas p58, Shutterstock/frenky362 p15(cr), Shutterstock/Ivan Galashchuk p49(tr), Shutterstock/Viktoria Gavrillina p40(cr), Shutterstock/Home Studio p120(paper), Shutterstock/infocus p50, Shutterstock/Iero p117, Shutterstock/isumi1 p55(b), Shutterstock/Mr.adisorn khiaopo p15(cm), Shutterstock/Lev Kropotov p6(tl), Shutterstock/Oleksandr Lysenko p41(cl), Shutterstock/Menna p26(bm), Shutterstock/Dmitry Naumaov p14, Shutterstock/Pavelis p25(cl), Shutterstock/Kristina Postnikova p49(tl), Shutterstock/Shuttertum p41(cml), Shutterstock/Zairo p63(tr); **Springer Nature Ltd** p120(pencil, ruler).

Printed and bound in Brazil

2022
14

Contents

Introducing *Max Science primary*

Max Science primary is a science course designed to meet the needs of learners following the Cambridge International Primary curriculum framework for Stages 1 to 6.

Success in science learning for young international learners and their teachers is enhanced through its practical approach to the skills of scientific enquiry and scientific vocabulary. Investigation and language activities in each unit progress learners from simple to more complex to make learning and understanding science accessible and fun.

The **Student Books** guide learners through key scientific knowledge, language and skills in the Cambridge curriculum. Each unit begins with an engaging introduction followed by activities that introduce and reinforce the skills of scientific enquiry, providing opportunities for learners to develop subject knowledge through investigation.

The **Workbooks** expand the key activities in each unit for use by the learners in pairs and groups in the classroom, or as individuals at home.

To further support the course, each stage has a **Journal** for use by learners at home, with the support of adults, to reinforce the knowledge and language of each topic. Teachers can review Journals at different points throughout the term to check progress at home against progress in school.

Also available are ***Max Science primary* Digital Student Books**, which offer an accompaniment to the more traditional printed Student Books. Ideal for encouraging digital literacy, these online books mirror the print course while offering extra interactive activities and assessment opportunities at home or in class.

Student Book features

Unit openers

Introduce the unit with clearly defined learning objectives, and stimulate interest with starter questions and images.

Orientation

Starter activities engage learners and help teachers assess how much the class already knows, before exploring further.

Key words

Key words for each section are clearly shown.

Interesting facts

Link science in the classroom to science in the real world.

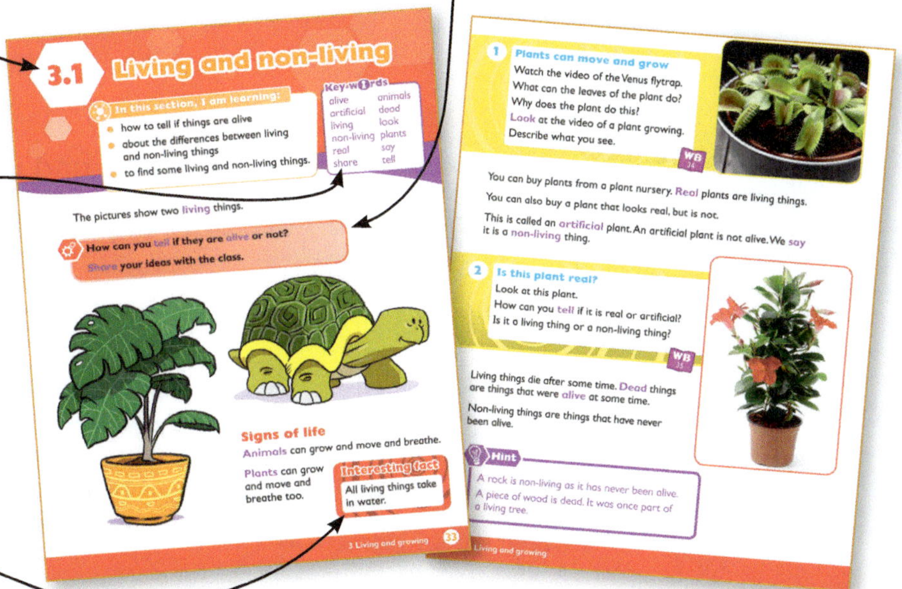

Exploring science

Investigations and extension questions help develop skills and understanding, and enable learners to predict, explore, test, measure, record and interpret scientific questions.

Workbook icon

Workbook icons in the Student Book direct teachers and learners to the corresponding activities in the Workbook.

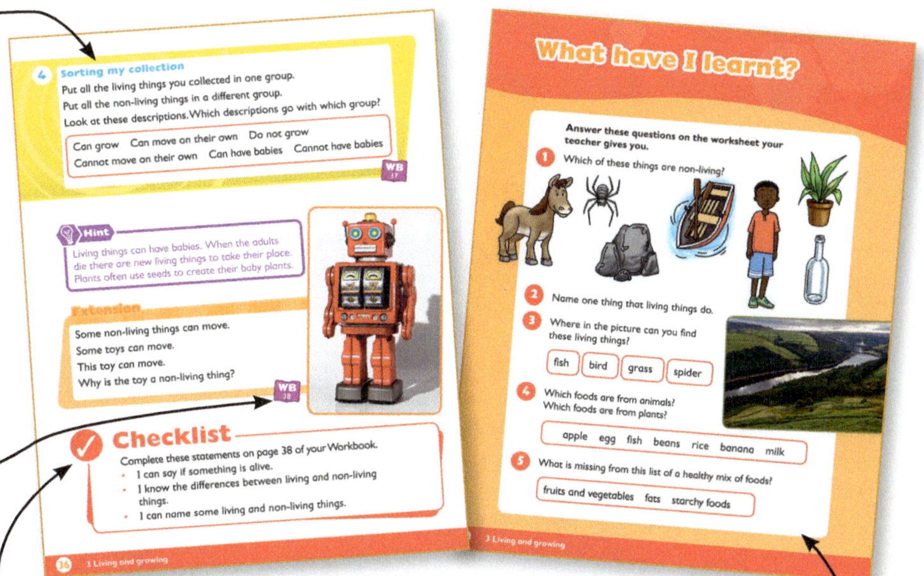

Assessing progress

End of topic checklists allow learners to check what they have learnt so far.

Cambridge Primary curriculum framework

In the spirit of the Cambridge Primary curriculum checkpoint tests, end of unit activities ask 'what have I learnt?' to sum up learners' progress in their learning journey so far.*

*See also the online versions at www.macmillaneducationeverywhere.com for downloading and printing with answer spaces provided.

1 The way we see things

Key words
light
shadow

In this unit, I am learning:

- how we see light sources and objects
- how we can use drawings to show where light travels
- which type of surfaces reflect light
- why a beam of light changes direction when it is reflected from a surface.

You should have already explored where light comes from. What can you remember?

1 Blocking light

a. Look at the photo. It shows a tennis player in Australia.

He is resting. He sits under a canopy to keep cool.

b. Working with a partner, use these words to explain why.

sun shade **light** **shadow**

WB 1

You are reading this page.
But how do you see the words and pictures?

2 How do we see things?

a. Tennis players can play in daytime matches or night-time under floodlights.

Look at the picture. It shows Daniel's ideas about seeing a tennis ball.

Can Daniel play tennis on a dark night without floodlights if this is true?

b. Work in pairs to finish the note to Daniel in your Workbook, explaining to him how seeing things works.

c. Do you all have the same ideas?

WB 2

1.1 Sources of light and seeing

Key words

explain, eyes, light, light source, object, show

In this section, I am learning:

- how light travels
- how we see things.

Sunlight

Anything that gives off its own **light** is called a **light source**.

Remember that our primary source of light is the Sun. Nuclear reactions release the Sun's energy and make it extremely hot.

The light from the Sun travels 150 million kilometres through space before it reaches Earth.

We see that light when it enters our **eyes**.

Talk with a partner about what appears to be happening in this photo of the Sun.

The Sun gives off light.

When you are inside a building in the daytime, the light from the Sun enters the rooms through any windows. The **objects** in a room with big windows are visible to us. But rooms with no windows to the outside appear dark and objects are difficult to see.

1

Modelling a sunny house

a. Working as a small group, make a cardboard model room to **show** a sunny house.

b. Darken the area around you. Now explore what happens inside the house when the torch is held in different positions.

Write down your observations in your Workbook.

c. **Explain** why a table in a bright room is visible to us, yet in a completely dark room we cannot see it.

WB 4

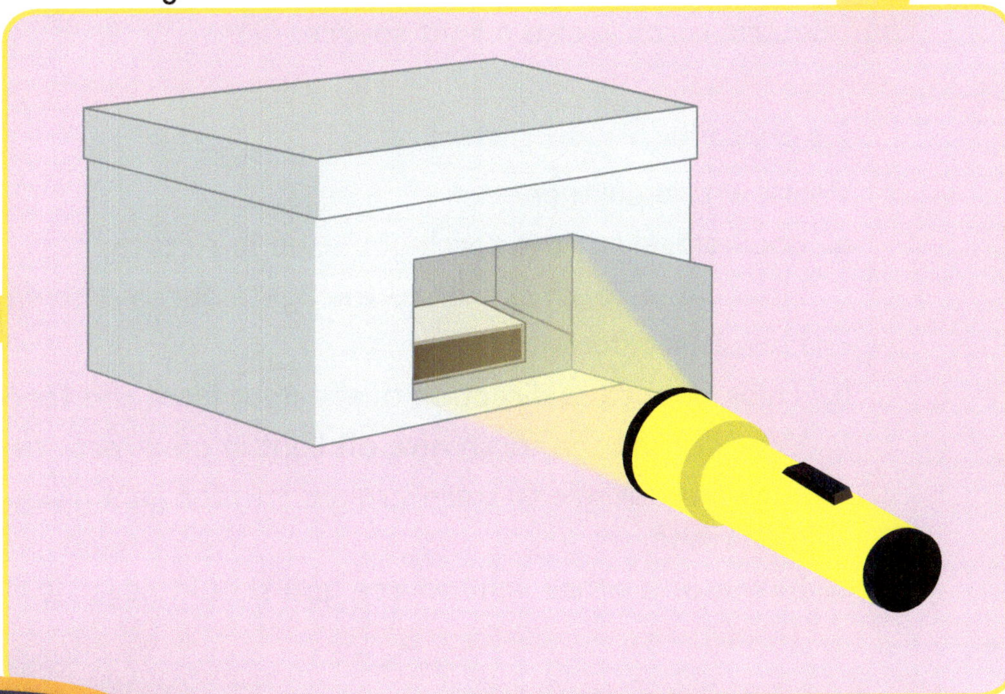

Discuss in your group, how you could change your model to test what you can see inside it when the cardboard window is closed.

Interesting fact

The Moon only reflects light from the Sun and so it is not a source of light.

Other sources of light

Any object that is hot enough to glow red (or even white) is a source of light.

Anything burning can also be a light source.

These things will give off light in all directions.

Your electric torch is also a light source.

2 Comparing light sources

Work with a partner.

a. Look closely at the torch you used in Activity 1.
- How is the torch similar to the light sources shown on this page?
- How is it different?

b. Think about the direction of the light from the torch.
- Why doesn't the torch give off light in all directions?
- Why is it not safe to stare straight into the light given off from the torch?

c. Name **one** other light source you should never look at directly.

WB 5

Does light move from the source to your eye or from your eye to the source?

Extension

In your Workbook, draw a diagram to show what you think happens to light when it passes from a bright light source through a pair of sunglasses.

WB 6

Interesting fact

The speed of light is 300 000 kilometres per second. Light from the Sun takes about 8 minutes to travel to Earth.

1.2 Rays of light

Key words

beam
opaque
predict
ray
shadow
translucent
transparent

In this section, I am learning:

- how shadows are formed
- how light travels
- how to represent rays of light travelling in drawings.

Making shadows

You have already looked at the **shadows** formed by objects.

The objects and materials that form the darkest shadows are **opaque**.

Opaque objects and materials do not let light pass through them. Wooden doors and brick walls are opaque.

Look at the tennis players. They are playing in a stadium with floodlights on at night.
How are the tennis players' shadows made?

1 Think about shadows

a. Write an explanation of the tennis players' shadows in your Workbook. Use these words:

light   floodlights   opaque   block

b. What do you think will happen to the shadows if two separate floodlights at one end of the stadium are turned off?

WB 7

Extension

Why can't you move faster than your shadow?

WB 8

Light travels through materials

Objects and materials that light can pass through are called **transparent**, for example glass windows.

Translucent materials let **some** light pass though.

Tracing paper is translucent, and so are frosted bathroom windows. So transparent materials let more light through than translucent materials.

Light travels in straight lines

Remember, shadows form because opaque objects block the light.

Light travels in straight lines and so it cannot bend around an object. The dark area behind the object where the light cannot reach is the shadow.

2 Exploring the path of light

a. With a partner, explain why Salim and Ravit can't see each other.

b. Can you think of a way to make the light change direction so Salim and Ravit can see around the corner?

What do you need to place at the corner?

c. **Predict** the path of the light and record your ideas in your Workbook.

WB 8

Showing where light travels

The light from a candle spreads out in all directions in straight lines.

To help us understand how we see things, we can draw a diagram.

Consider one observer. The light travelling into his eye can be shown by a single straight line.

We call this straight line a **ray** or **beam** of light. The arrow shows the direction the light is travelling.

Extension

A boy can see two candles burning at the end of a table. They are 20 cm apart.

Draw a ray diagram in your Workbook to show how the boy can see both candles.

WB 9

Checklist

Complete the checklist on page 9 in your Workbook.

- I know some light sources.
- I know how we can see a light source.
- I can explain how shadows are formed.
- I know that light travels in straight lines.
- I can draw rays of light on a ray diagram.

1.3 Mirrors

In this section, I am learning:

- that rays of light can be reflected by surfaces, including mirrors
- how reflected light enters our eyes so we can see an object
- some uses of mirrors.

Key words

discuss
image
mirror
object
observe
ray diagram
record
reflect
surface

Changing the direction of light

When light rays hit an **object**, they can 'bounce' off the **surface** of the object and travel in a new direction. We call this reflection.

How do mirrors affect the path of light rays?

1 Check yourself out

a. Look at yourself in a **mirror**. **Discuss** with a partner why it is possible to see yourself in a mirror.

b. We call the picture you see in a mirror 'an **image**'. It is a mirror image of you.

Do you think the image is still there in a totally dark room?

WB 10

Hint

Remember that rays of light **do not** travel out of your eyes!

We can see what new clothes look like on us before we buy them by looking in a mirror.

2 **Mirror writing**

a. Write your name on a piece of paper and hold the paper in front of the mirror. In your Workbook, copy the image of your name that you see in the mirror.

b. Working in pairs, discuss how you can make an image of your name that looks the same as the way you wrote it. Try out your idea.

Hint
A second mirror will help you with this.

c. How is the image of an object seen in the mirror the same as the real object? How is it different? **Record** these observations.

WB 11

Why can we see an accurate image of an object in a mirror?

How mirrors work

Light from an object bounces off the smooth, shiny surface of a mirror. We say that the rays of light are '**reflected**' from the surface of the mirror.

We see the reflected light rays and they appear to have come from behind the mirror. We can see an image that we think is behind the mirror.

This can be shown on a **ray diagram**.

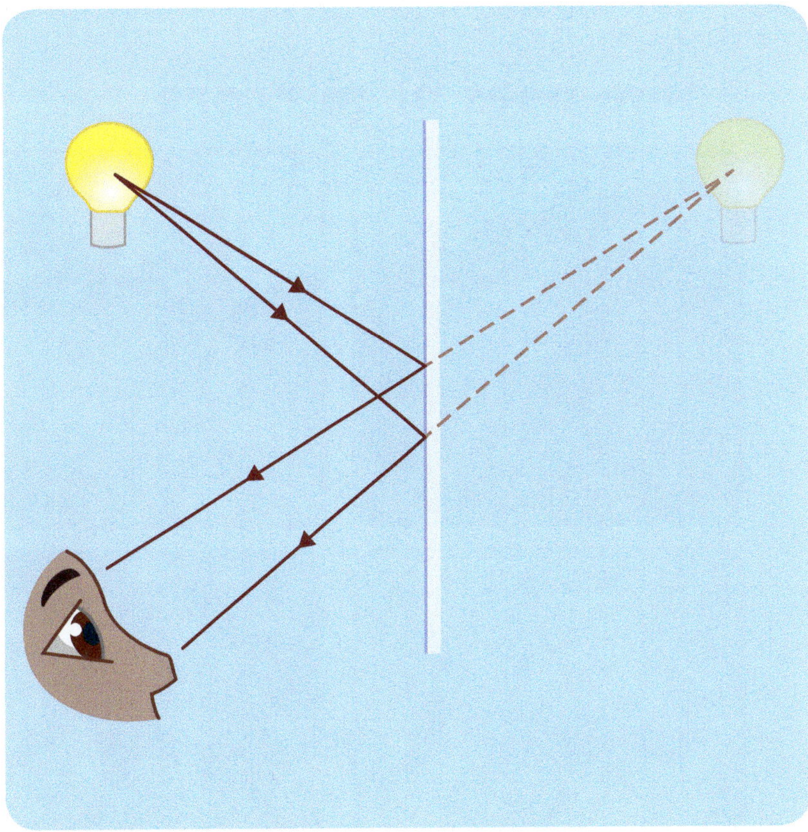

3 Investigating reflection

Work in small groups.

a. You will need a ray box and a mirror. With the room lights dimmed, learn how to make a single beam of light using the ray box.

b. Direct the single beam to a mirror standing in a holder. The mirror should be vertical. **Observe** what happens to the beam.

WB 11

Hint

Don't forget to put arrows on the light rays you draw to show their direction.

Some uses of mirrors

1

2

3

4

4 How we can use mirrors

a. Talk with a partner about how the mirrors in these photos are used.

b. Write a sentence explaining how we use each of these mirrors or draw a diagram showing light rays to help explain each use.

WB 12

Periscopes

Remember, when a light ray hits a mirror it changes direction.

This property of mirrors helps us to see things that are out of our 'line of sight', for example, objects around a corner or over a wall.

Without using mirrors, we cannot see the object because light rays only travel in straight lines and cannot bend.

Look at the people watching a golf match. Some of them are using periscopes. Periscopes are tubes or long boxes containing two mirrors. We use periscopes to see out of our line of sight. The mirrors change the direction of the light rays so they can reach our eyes.

Why are these people looking into long boxes?

Submarines also use periscopes. They use them to see what is happening above the surface of the sea without showing themselves. They can remain hidden beneath the sea.

5 Up periscope!

a. Why do periscopes contain two mirrors?

b. Discuss with a partner how someone with a periscope in a submarine beneath the surface of the water can see a bird on a nearby island.

WB 13

6 Designing a periscope

Work in small groups or pairs.

a. Design your own periscope in your Workbook. You can use two small mirrors and a long cardboard box, such as a shoe box or a cereal box.

Look at Tarla's periscope to give you some ideas.

b. If you have time, make the periscope and test if it works!

WB 14

Tarla's periscope.

Hint

The mirrors in your periscope should be at an angle of 45 degrees.

Extension

A laser beam is a powerful and narrow beam of light.

Find out one use of lasers.

WB 14

Interesting fact

Scientists on Earth directed a laser at a mirror left on the moon by NASA astronauts and collected the reflected laser beam. They used this information to measure the distance from the Earth to the Moon.

1.4 Investigating light

In this section, I am learning:

- to investigate which surfaces reflect light best
- what makes a good reflector of light
- that a light meter can be used to investigate light.

Key words

conclusion
evaluate
factor
fair test
investigate
line graph
measure
plan
reliable
repeat
variable

Remember – light travels in straight lines and mirrors reflect light. What other factors affect the path of light?

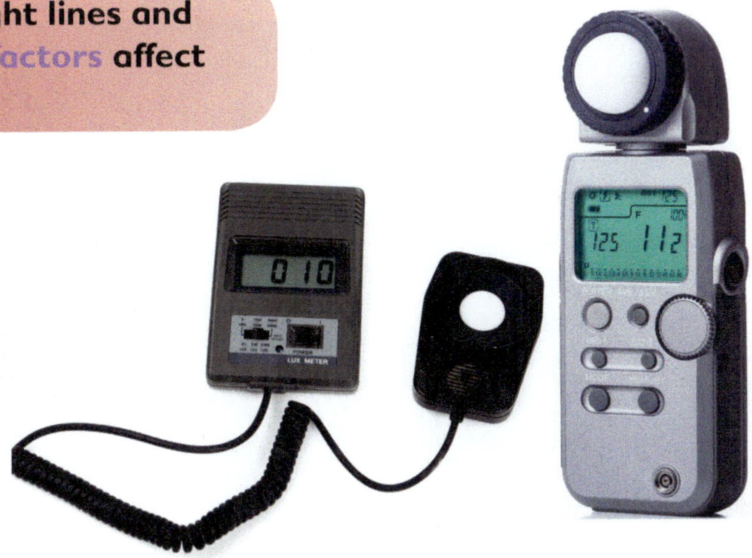

Measuring brightness

A light meter can be used to accurately **measure** the brightness of light. A light meter reads in units of Lux.

A light meter can be used in different types of investigations of light.

1 Using a light meter

Work in small groups.

Investigate the following questions.

a. How does the brightness of light from a torch change the further away it is?

b. How much light is reflected from the surface of a mirror?

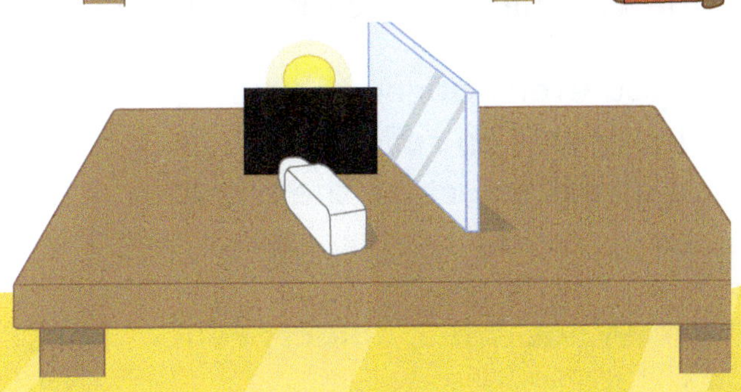

cont …

c. How much light passes through a piece of tracing or tissue paper?

Write about your discoveries in your Workbook. Draw a **line graph** to show your results.

WB 15

Interesting fact

Cricket umpires use light meters to judge whether the light is bright enough to keep playing.

What makes a good reflector?

Some objects and materials make good reflectors. You looked at mirrors in section 1.3. Mirrors are made of glass.

Have you ever noticed the sunlight reflecting off a glass window? If the window is at just the right angle to reflect the light from an object into your eyes, you can see a mirror image of the object on the window.

What other objects reflect light? What are they made from?

2 Which surfaces make the best reflectors of light?

Work in pairs.

a. You are going to investigate which surfaces reflect light best without using a light meter.

- How will you **plan** to make your investigation a **fair test**?
- What things (**variables**) will you keep the same when testing each material?

b. Shine a torch onto different materials. Using just your eyes, judge the brightness of the light bouncing off.

Repeat the test with pairs of materials until you can put them in order from best to worst reflector.

c. What **conclusion** can you make about good and bad reflectors of light?

d. **Evaluate** your investigation. Discuss the **reliability** of your investigation with your partner.

- Can you trust the results and your conclusion?
- What improvements could you make?

WB 16

Hint

It is difficult to order materials from best reflector to worst reflector using just your eyes to judge brightness. Try testing two materials at the same time, next to each other. Then you can see which of the two reflects the brighter light.

Rough or smooth?

A smooth surface is a better reflector of light than a rough surface.

Rough surfaces scatter the light rays in all directions.

This means that smooth surfaces look shiny, and rougher surfaces look duller.

Shiny and smooth materials such as glass, metals and glazed ceramics (for example shiny tiles) are good reflectors of light, but rough, dull surfaces are not.

These ray diagrams help to explain why this is.

The smooth surface reflects light in a uniform way. The rough surface causes the reflected light to be scattered.

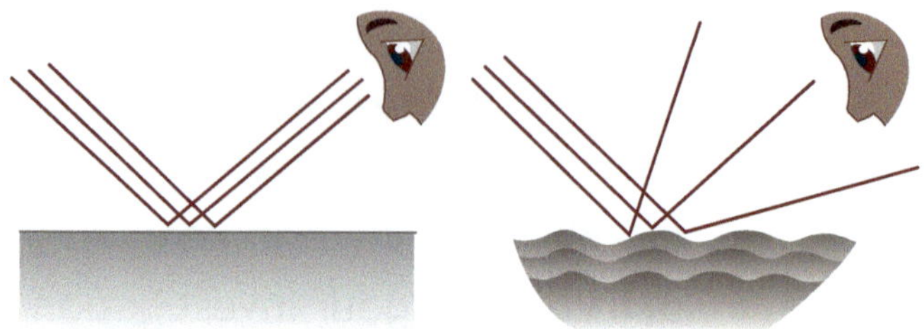

3 A bright classroom

Work in small groups.

a. Choose materials to make a bright classroom.

Draw your design in your Workbook and label the materials.

b. Explain how each of your choices will make the classroom as bright as possible in natural light.

WB 17

Extension

Discuss how you could use a light meter to improve the reliability of your reflector investigation in Activity 2.

WB 18

✓ Checklist

Complete the checklist on page 18 in your Workbook.

- I can show how rays of light can be reflected by surfaces.
- I know how we can see a reflection of an object.
- I can describe some uses of mirrors.
- I can describe and explain what makes a good reflector of light.
- I can investigate the brightness of light and its reflection.

What have I learnt?

Answer these questions on the worksheet your teacher gives you.

1 **A piece of black card with a small hole cut in it is placed in front of a torch.**

The torch is shone onto a block of wood.

a Draw rays of light on a diagram like the one above, to show how a shadow forms on the screen. Label the area in shadow.

b Explain how the shadow from the block of wood forms.

c Name the light source in the experiment above.

d How would the results of the experiment be different if the block was made of glass instead of wood?

2 **Nissa can see the reflection of a light bulb in a mirror.**

a Draw a ray of light on a diagram like thisone to show how Nissa can see the light bulb.

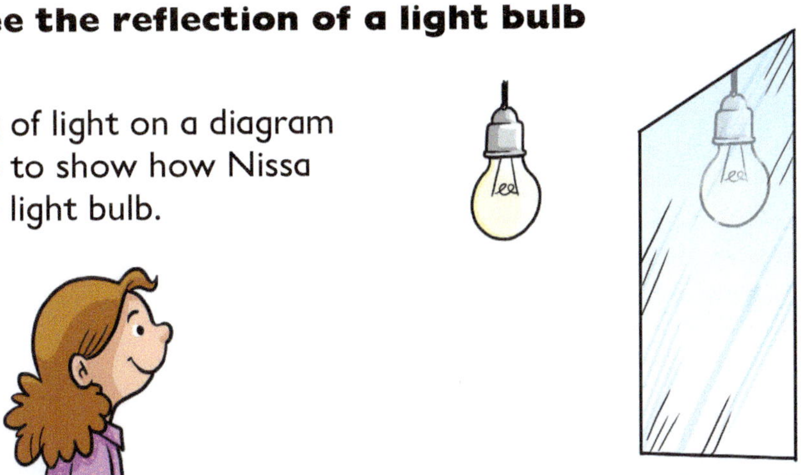

b What are the two missing words below?
The light from the bulb is _?_ by the _?_ surface of the mirror.

3 **Sam and Tami investigated which of these four materials are good reflectors of light.**

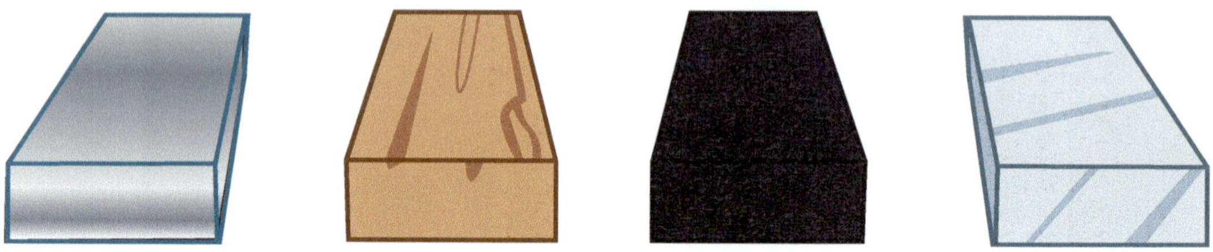

aluminium wood rubber glass

They used a torch and a ruler.

a How did Sam and Tami use the ruler to make their investigation a fair test?

b Put the four materials in order of their ability to reflect light, with the best reflector first.

c Describe two things that good reflectors of light have in common.

2 Evaporation and condensation

In this unit, I am learning:

- about the evaporation of liquids
- about the condensation of gases
- how water is recycled in nature
- how to remove insoluble solids from a liquid.

Key words

gas
liquid
particles
solid
state of matter

You have learnt about solids, liquids and gases, and explored a variety of materials. What can you remember?

1 Linking key words

a. Work in pairs to discuss these questions.

- What do we call water when it is **solid**?
- What do we call the water that rises from a kettle of boiling water as a **gas**?

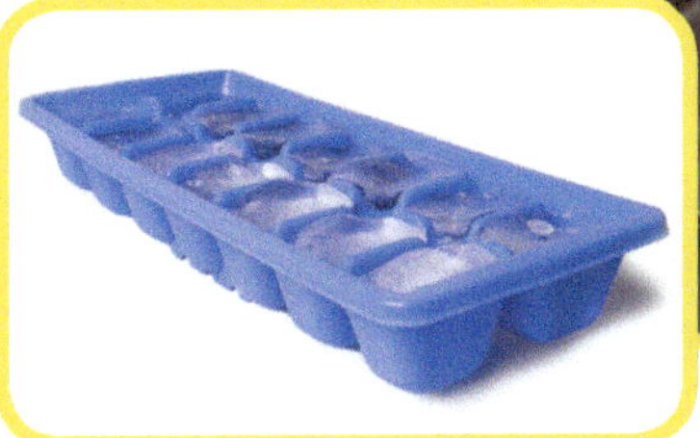

b. Draw a mind map to link the words in this box.

water steam **liquid**
ice gas solid

c. Swap mind maps with your partner.

- How are they similar?
- How are they different?

d. Amira wants to make links between more words. She suggests the words in this box:

kettle pour drip cold

- What connections can you find between these words?
- Can you add some more words of your own?

WB 20

Modelling states of matter

In science we sometimes explain ideas using models.

What do you think makes a good model?

Everything you can see is made up of something. In science we call this matter. Matter can be a solid, a liquid or a gas.

Can you name two solids, two liquids and two gases?

Solid, liquid and gas are called the three **states of matter**.

Scientists believe that all matter is made up of tiny **particles** that are too small to see.

If the particles in matter are too small to see, we can use a model to help us understand them.

This is not a real train, it is a model.

2 Modelling solids, liquids and gases

Work in groups.

a. Discuss the properties of solids, liquids and gases.

b. Imagine that you are all tiny particles of a material in a human 'model of matter'.

How are you arranged and how do you move in:

- a solid
- a liquid
- a gas?

c. Show another group your ideas. Watch them model a solid, a liquid and a gas.

d. Discuss your models.

WB 21

2.1 Evaporation

In this section, I am learning:

- what 'evaporation' means
- some examples of evaporation
- what happens to the particles in a liquid when it evaporates.

Key words

bar chart
evaporation
evidence
factors
fair test
gas
interpret data
investigate
line graph
liquid
measure
observe
particles
prediction
reliable
variable
water vapour

When it rains heavily we get puddles of water on the ground.
But the puddles do not stay there forever.
What happens to the water in puddles?

Puddles form after heavy rain.

1 Where do all the puddles go?

a. What happens to the size of a puddle when the Sun comes out?

- Write a **prediction** in your Workbook.
- Explain why you think this will happen.

b. With a partner, plan an **investigation** to find out what happens. You have a measuring tape and a stop clock.

c. What type of graph is best to show the pattern of your results?
A **bar chart** or a **line graph**?
Explain your choice.

WB 22

Extension

a. Carry out your investigation from Activity 1. If there are no puddles outside, place a saucer of water near a radiator or on a sunny windowsill to measure instead.

b. Record your results in a table in your Workbook.

If you have enough measurements you can draw a line graph. Put 'Distance across water in cm' up the side (you will need to read this to the nearest mm). Put 'Time in hours' across the bottom of your graph.

c. Interpret your results and write a conclusion in your Workbook.

WB 23

Liquid into gas

When you heat a liquid it will eventually become a **gas**. We call this **evaporation**. If the **particles** that make up the liquid have enough energy, they can escape from the liquid's surface.

Usually, you can't see the gas escaping from a liquid as it evaporates. However, sometimes, in very hot conditions, you can see this water (called **water vapour**) rising from plant life or ground that has been soaked in rain.

When the weather is described as 'humid', the air contains a lot of water vapour.

In hot conditions, you can see rainwater evaporating into the air. This makes the air humid.

Interesting fact

Hawkmoths feed on plant nectar. Water evaporates from plant nectar causing small increases in humidity, which are detected by the hawkmoths. This helps them to choose which plants they can get nectar from.

2 Warming water

a. Watch your teacher heat a pan of water on a hot plate.

- What do you notice, or **observe**, above the water before it boils?
- Discuss your observation with a partner.

b. Explain your observation using the word 'particles'.

WB 24

Other examples of evaporation

We can make use of liquids that evaporate easily.

Some liquids, such as perfumes and aftershave, give off nice smells when they evaporate. You cannot see the particles of the perfume evaporating. But you do know that some of the particles have entered your nose because you can smell them.

This is **evidence** that liquids are made of tiny invisible particles.

Other liquids that evaporate easily are used as fuels, such as petrol. You probably know the smell of petrol from petrol stations.

Perfume evaporates easily.

Why is it dangerous to strike a match in a petrol station?

3 That smells nice!

Watch your teacher warm some scented oil (oil containing perfume) using a tealight candle.

a. Who smells the oil first?

b. What do you notice about their position in the room?

c. Write about what is happening in the room as the oil warms up. Include details about the particles, the air and the perfume.

WB 24

4 What makes washing dry more quickly?

Work in small groups.

a. Discuss and list the **factors** (**variables**) that affect how quickly washing will dry.

b. Choose one variable from your list to investigate.

- You can model the wind and different temperatures with a hairdryer.
- You can use a piece of cloth or fabric, such as a handkerchief, to model your washing.

c. Plan a **fair test** to see how your chosen variable affects the time it takes your washing to dry.

- Which variables will you keep the same in each test? How will you do this?
- How will you judge how quickly the washing is drying?

d. Carry out your investigation.

- If you have a sensitive electric balance you can check the mass of the washing at different times. If not, you can use your observations and judgement rather than measurements.
- Record your observations in your Workbook.

e. Write down your conclusion. Make sure you mention 'evaporation'.

f. Discuss your investigation with your group.

- How can you improve the investigation to make the results more **reliable**?
- Do you need to repeat each test?

WB 25

Extension

The pictures show two ways to hang your washing out to dry.

Mrs Khanduri used to hang her washing on a long line. Then she bought a new rotary drier.

a. The washing dried faster on the old, long line. Can you explain why?

b. What is the advantage of the rotary drier?

WB 26

A long washing line

A rotary drier

2.2 Condensation

In this section, I am learning:

- what happens when water vapour meets a cold surface
- some examples of condensation
- what happens to the particles in a gas when the gas condenses.

Keywords

condensation
condense
gas
liquid
observe

Why does liquid appear on some cold surfaces?

Have you ever noticed drops of **liquid** on the outside of a cold drinks can or bottle when you take it out of the fridge? What about the inside of a window getting wet?

What do you think this liquid is? Where does it come from?

1 Talking about condensation

a. Kassim and his friends are drinking fizzy drinks. They discuss the **condensation** on the outside of the cold cans.

b. Which of their ideas do you agree with?

WB 27

2 Observing condensation

Watch your teacher boil a kettle of water and then hold a mirror above the kettle's spout.

a. Write down your **observations** in your Workbook.

b. What do you think happens on the surface of the mirror? Write about the 'particles of water' and the changing temperature.

WB 27

3 Surface temperature affects condensation

Zara's teacher tried the experiment in Activity 2 with a warm mirror. She didn't really see any condensation. Why is there more condensation on a cold mirror?

WB 28

The change of state when a kettle boils

Gas into liquid

Remember, there are large spaces between the particles that make up **gases**. These gas particles can zoom around very quickly. They bounce off each other when they bump together.

As we cool a gas, the energy in the particles decreases and they slow down. When the gas is cool enough, some particles clump together and form drops. This is when liquid starts to form.

At this point, we say that the gas is condensing.

Sometimes condensation is described as the opposite (or reverse) of evaporation.

Extension

Work in pairs.

a. Can you explain evaporation to your partner? Write a definition in your Workbook.

b. Can you explain and define condensation?

c. Produce a labelled drawing to explain evaporation and condensation.

WB 28

Checklist

Complete the checklist on page 29 in your Workbook.

- I can describe what "evaporation" and "condensation" mean.
- I can list some examples of evaporation and condensation.
- I can describe what happens to the particles in a liquid when it evaporates.
- I can investigate and understand what affects the drying of clothes on a washing line.
- I can describe what happens to the particles in a gas when the gas condenses.

2.3 The water cycle

In this section, I am learning:

- that in nature, water is recycled
- to explain the water cycle including changes of state of water
- to investigate evaporation from surfaces with different areas.

Keywords

condensation
condense
evaporation
evaporate
fair test
state of matter
variable
water cycle

The journey of water

Have you ever wondered where clouds come from or how rain forms?

In this section, you can use your understanding about **evaporation** and **condensation** to explain what happens to water in nature. You will also revise melting and freezing.

These are rain clouds. You can read more about clouds on page 33.

1 Clouds

Ling and her friends are not happy. It is raining and they must stay inside. They start talking about clouds.

Work in small groups.

a. Discuss the ideas in the picture.

b. Sort the ideas into three groups in your Workbook.

c. Discuss the ideas with your teacher and the rest of the class.

WB 30

Nature's water cycle

In nature, water is constantly recycled. We call this the **water cycle**.

Look at the diagram of the water cycle.

It shows five stages in the recycling of water.

2 Flow diagram water cycle

a. What are the changes in the **state of matter** of water in the water cycle? Organise them into a simple flow diagram in your Workbook.

b. Discuss your flow diagram with a partner. Do you need to make any changes?

WB 31

3 Daniel's bathtime

It is winter and very cold outside. Daniel decides to take a nice hot bath to warm up. He closes the bathroom window and runs hot water into the bath.

After his bath, he wipes the water off the mirror with his towel so he can see his reflection. He also notices that the tiles on the wall feel wet.

Compare the water cycle in nature to Daniel's bathtime. Can the water cycle happen in Daniel's bathroom? Discuss your ideas in a group.

WB 31

Investigating evaporation

In the water cycle, water evaporates from the surface of the sea. But water also evaporates into the air from any source of water. This includes ponds, lakes, streams and rivers.

4 Does the surface area affect how fast water evaporates?

Work in small groups.

a. Choose four different shapes of container that you can fill with water.

Label the containers A to D.

Draw the containers in your Workbook.

b. Write a prediction in your Workbook.

- From which container will water evaporate fastest?
- Put the containers in order (put the fastest evaporation first).
- Explain your choices.

c. Plan your investigation.

- How will you make this a **fair test**?
- How will you measure how much water has evaporated after a set time (for example, two days)?

Hint

Measure and record the volume of the water at the start. Repeat this measurement after a few days.

d. Carry out your investigation and record the results in your Workbook. Will you display your results for containers A to D on a line graph or a bar chart?

Hint

List the four containers (labelled A to D) across the bottom of your graph. Do you have named **variables** (shown on bar charts) or measured variables (shown on line graphs)?

e. Look back at your results. Was the prediction you made correct?

WB 32

Interesting fact

Clouds come in many different shapes and sizes.

We get different cloud formations because of their varying heights and temperatures.

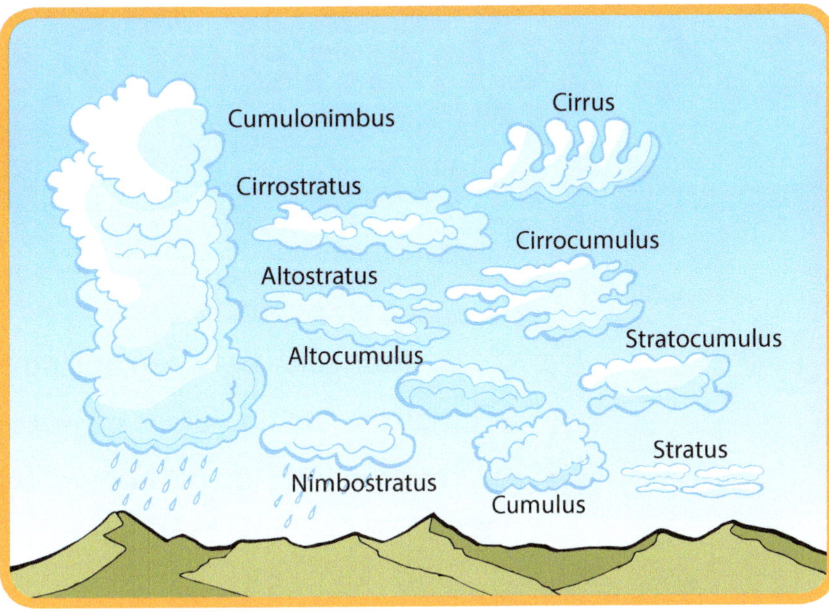

Extension

Look at these 'Changes of state' flow diagrams. Which two changes of state are caused by water cooling down? What causes clouds to rise and cool down?

WB 35

Liquid water in sea
↓ **Evaporation**
Water vapour (gas) in air
↓ **Condensation**
Liquid water

Droplets in clouds
↓ **Freezing**
Solid ice crystals in clouds

Clouds

The highest clouds have the lowest temperatures. They are made of tiny ice crystals.

The lowest clouds are warmest. They are made of small droplets of liquid water.

✓ Checklist

Complete the checklist on page 35 in your Workbook.

- I can describe the water cycle that occurs in nature.
- I can explain the stages of the water cycle, including any changes of state.
- I can use the idea of water particles when explaining the water cycle.

2.4 Changing the state of water

Keywords

boiling point
line graph
melting point
particles
water vapour

In this section, I am learning:

- to distinguish between boiling and evaporation
- that the melting point of water is 0 °C
- that the boiling point of water is 100 °C.

Why are some foods cooked in boiling water?

Hint

Think about biting an uncooked rice grain or a raw root vegetable. What happens to them after they are boiled in water?

Many people eat rice boiled in water as an important part of their diet.

1 Cooking food and making drinks

Answer these questions and compare your answers with a partner's.

a. Which foods do you boil in water before eating? Make a list in your Workbook.

b. Which drinks are made with boiling water?

c. Why is boiling water used to make these drinks rather than cold water?

WB 36

2 Observing boiling water

Watch your teacher heat a pan of water until it starts to boil.

a. What do you see happening as the water boils? Write a description in your Workbook.

b. Watch your teacher measure the temperature of the boiling water (in degrees celsius, °C) using a thermometer. This temperature is called the **boiling point**.

Record the boiling point of water in your Workbook.

WB 36

Discuss with a partner how boiling compares with evaporation. How is it the same? How is it different?

Boiling and particles

When a liquid boils it changes its state to a gas. Water boils at a boiling point of 100 °C.

When a liquid boils, large bubbles form within the liquid. They rise rapidly through the liquid and burst out from its surface. The bubbles are made up of **water vapour**.

> **Hint**
> We can describe both 'boiling' and 'evaporation' as a liquid changing its state to a gas – **but evaporation can happen at temperatures lower than the boiling point.**

Remember that in general:

1. The bubbles that form when a liquid boils are **not empty space** and they do not contain air. They contain **particles** from the boiling liquid.
2. The particles in the liquid state of a material and the particles in the gaseous state of the same material are the **same** particles. It is the movement and distance between particles that change as the liquid boils.
   - The particles in a gas travel much faster than those in a liquid.
   - The particles in a gas have much more space between each other than those in a liquid.

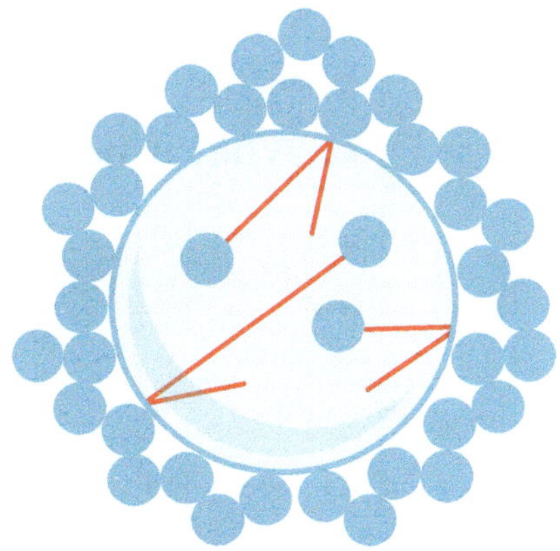

This shows the water particles in and around a bubble in boiling water.

Melting point of water

When ice melts and turns into liquid water, it is at its **melting point**.

Ice melts at the same temperature as water freezes.

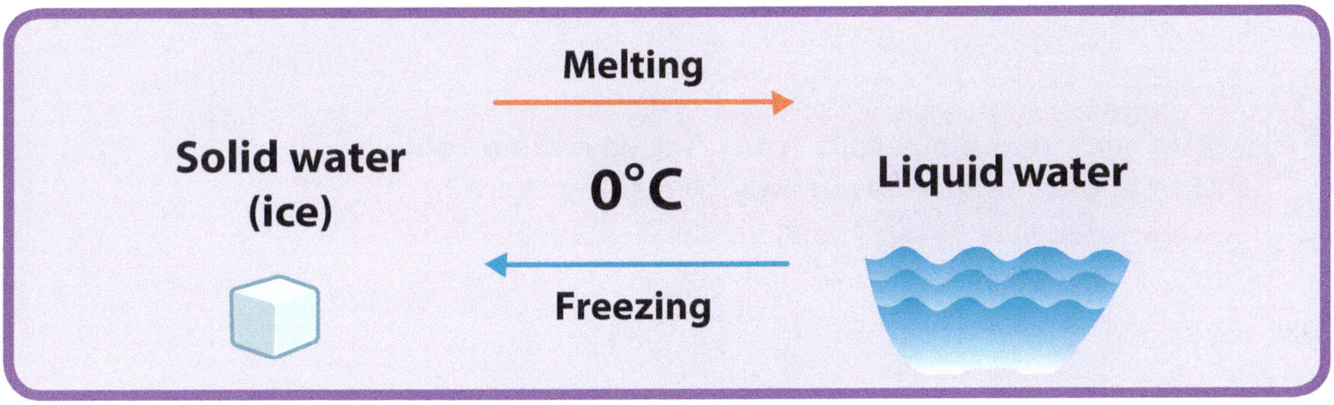

3 Melting ice

Work in pairs.

Set up your experiment:

- Collect several ice cubes in a plastic beaker.
- Measure the temperature of the frozen ice.
- As the ice melts, you will see water and ice mixed together. Measure the temperature as the ice melts into water – this is the melting point. This will take about an hour.

Record your answers to the following questions in your Workbook.

a. What is the melting point of water in °C?

b. What is the freezing point of water in °C?

c. What is happening to the water particles in the ice cubes as the ice melts?

WB 37

4 What happens to the temperature of water as it is heated?

Watch your teacher measure the temperature of water as it is heated up to its boiling point.

We can use a thermometer to measure the temperature every one or two minutes.

You can use a temperature sensor instead if your school has one.

a. Record each temperature the teacher measures in your Workbook.

b. What happened to the temperature once the water started to boil?

WB 37

You recorded the results from Activity 4 in a table. Can you think of another way to display them?

Line graphs

In science, we use **line graphs** to display the results of an investigation when both of the variables are measured. (This means that they are both shown as numbers).

The data in Activity 4 are both sets of measured numbers, e.g. 2 mins and 20 °C.

When drawing a line graph, make sure:

- you label both axes, including units
- your scales go up evenly
- you plot the points with small, neat crosses, x, using a sharp pencil.

Here is an example of how measurements can be used to make a point on a graph.

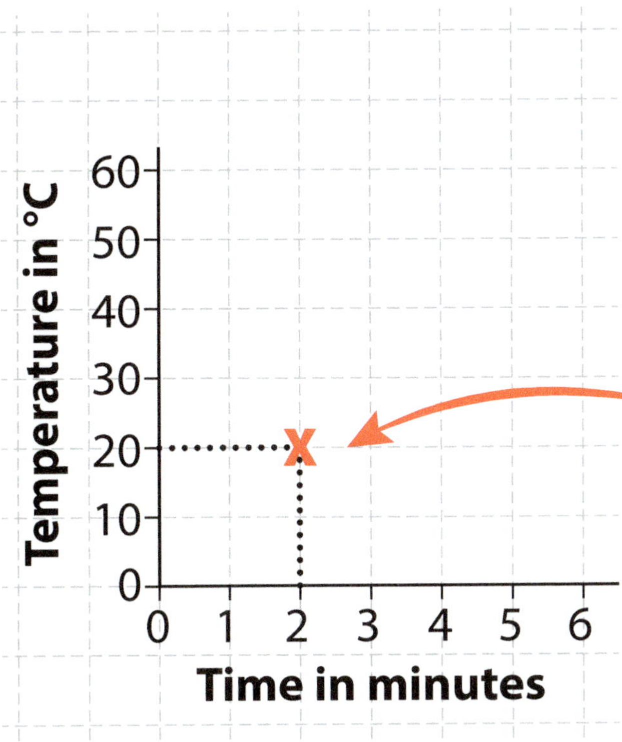

Time in minutes	Temperature in °C
2	20

5 Drawing line graphs

In your Workbook, complete the graph to show your results from Activity 4.

WB 38

Here is an example of a line graph showing results from heating water to its boiling point.

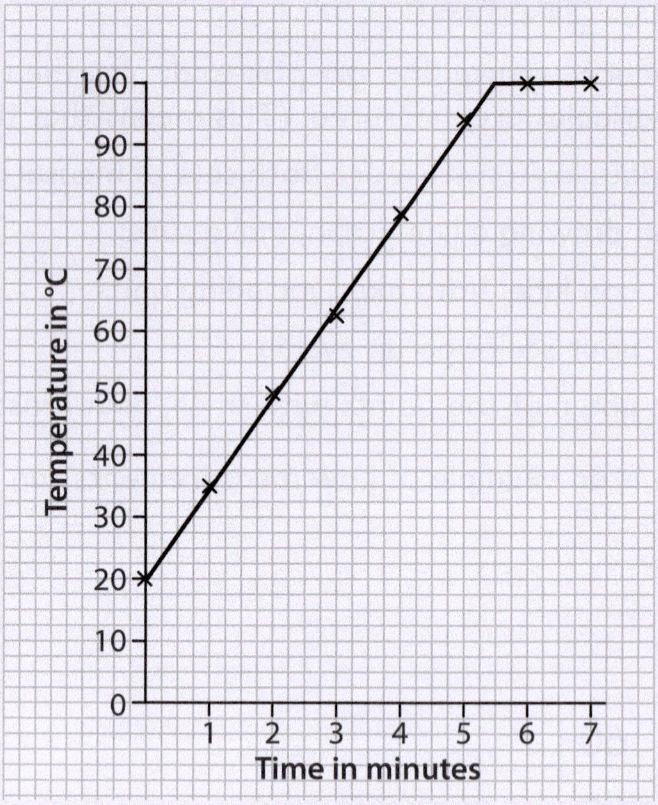

Extension

Look at the line graph above.

a. What was the water temperature after five minutes?

b. What was the temperature of the room at the start of the experiment? How did you work this out?

c. How long did it take for the water to boil?

d. Was the water heated steadily as the temperature was rising? How can you tell?

e. If the water is heated for five minutes more, what do you think the temperature will be? Malik said 120 °C. Rhianna said 100 °C. What do you think? Discuss your ideas with a partner.

WB 38

Checklist

Complete the checklist on page 39 in your Workbook.

- I can tell the difference between boiling and evaporation.
- I know the melting point of water.
- I know the boiling point of water.

2.5 Making and separating solutions

In this section, I am learning:

- to test whether materials are soluble or insoluble
- to separate a mixture of materials by sieving or filtering
- to collect a solid from a solution.

Keywords

apparatus
crystals
evaporate
fair test
filter funnel
filter paper
insoluble
particles
prediction/predict
sieve
solid
soluble
solution

Dissolving

Remember – some materials dissolve in water but others do not.

- The materials that dissolve in water are described as **soluble**.
- The mixture of the dissolved material and water is called a **solution**.
- Materials that do not dissolve in water are described as **insoluble**.

Powders are fine specks of **solid** material. Some are soluble and some are insoluble in water. If you stir a powder into water and the mixture looks cloudy, some solid bits have not dissolved.

1 Soluble or insoluble powders?

Work in small groups.

a. Plan a test to see if some powders are soluble or insoluble. Show your plan to your teacher to check.

b. Try out the tests on the powders provided. Record your findings in your Workbook.

WB 40

Hint

Think about these things: How much water will you use? Will you need a cup or a beaker? Will you need more than one beaker? Will you use a spoon to stir? How will you tell when a material has dissolved?

When a material dissolves in water it seems to disappear, but it doesn't. The material's **particles** mix completely with the water particles but the particles of the solid are still in the solution. Remember – the individual particles that make up any material are too small for us to see.

Extension

a. Using what you know about particles, explain how sugar dissolves in water.

b. Why does sugar seem to disappear when it dissolves?

c. How can you prove that the sugar is still there in the sugar solution? Discuss your ideas with a partner and see if you can think of two ways.

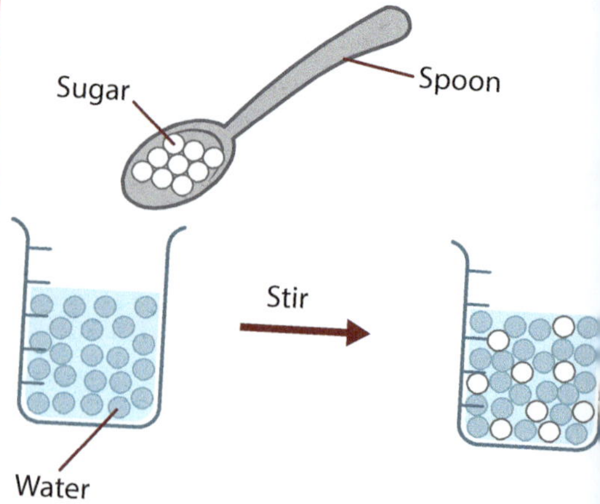

WB 41

Separation in action – making coffee

Coffee is a very popular hot drink. It is made from coffee beans. They are grown in countries with warm, sunny weather.

Brazil, Kenya and Ethiopia are famous for growing coffee beans. They send their beans all around the world.

Coffee beans from the plant are green in colour before roasting.

Coffee beans can be different sizes. They can be separated out to make more expensive coffee. **Sieves** can be used to sort the beans into three sizes – small, medium and large.

Coffee beans are sorted by size in Kenya using sieves.

2 Sorting coffee beans

Work in pairs.

a. Design a machine that can sort coffee beans into three different sizes.

b. Show your design to another pair, and find out about their ideas.

c. Can you improve your design to make a better machine? Draw your improved design on a large piece of paper to show others in your classroom.

WB 42

Filtering ground-up coffee

When coffee beans have been roasted, they can be ground up to make coffee powder. With powder, you can get the full flavour of the coffee more quickly. The taste of coffee comes from materials in the beans. These materials dissolve in hot water.

The soluble materials that give coffee its flavour pass through **filter paper** in the **filter funnel**. The flask collects the coffee solution. The insoluble bits of the ground-up coffee beans are left in the filter paper.

Filtering coffee

The technique of filtration

Making coffee to drink is an example of how insoluble material can be separated from soluble materials.

Scientists also use filtration to separate materials.

Look at this **apparatus**:

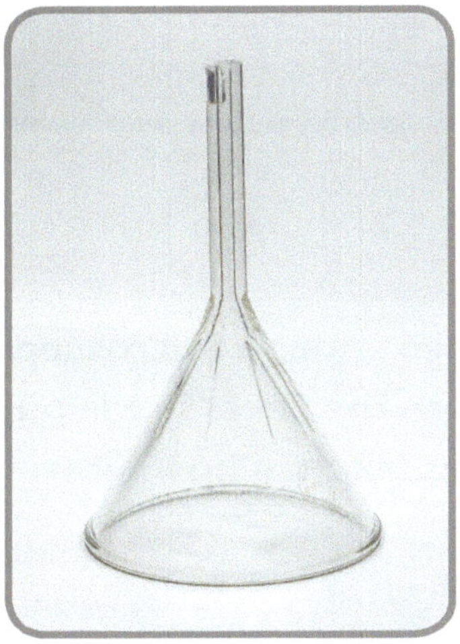

Apparatus that can be used to filter a mixture in a science laboratory

We can draw this apparatus in a scientific diagram like this:

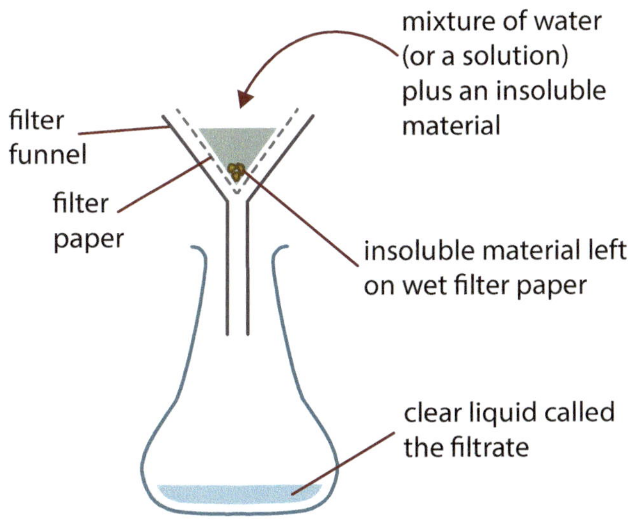

A scientific diagram of filtration

Compare the photo with the scientific diagram. What does the diagram show?

3 Filtering muddy water

Work in pairs.

a. Filter muddy water using a filter funnel and filter paper.

b. Repeat the filtering process until you get a clear solution.

c. Draw a scientific diagram of your experiment in your Workbook.

WB 42

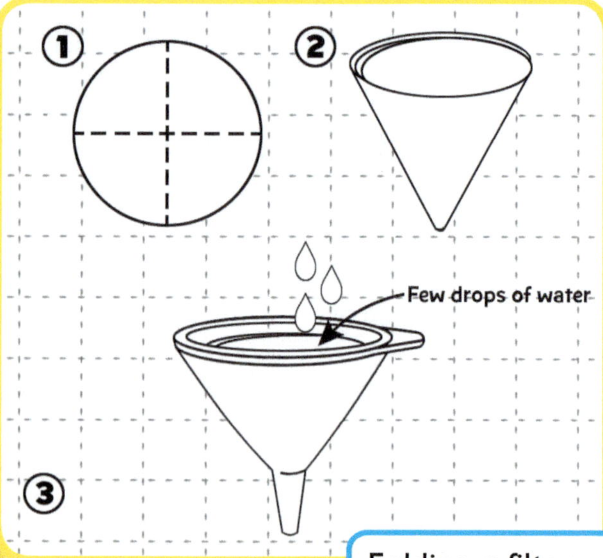

Folding a filter paper and fitting it in a filter funnel

Hint

Remember:

- Do not fill the filter paper cone in the funnel above its top or let any muddy water go behind the filter paper – the solution **must** pass through the filter paper.
- Do not poke or stir the muddy water in the filter paper cone in case you tear the filter paper – then the muddy water will just run straight through.

Extension

Look at this piece of filter paper viewed under a microscope.

Filter paper has very tiny gaps between the fibres in the paper.

Using what you know about particles, explain how filtering can make muddy water clear.

WB 43

Hint

Think of the filter paper like a very fine sieve.

Interesting fact

Sewage works use filtration to help clean waste water. Instead of filter paper, the dirty water passes through layers of small stones and sand. This filters out small bits of insoluble solid waste from the water.

Evaporating solutions

Salt dissolves in water. It becomes a salt solution.

To get the solid salt back from the solution, we need to **evaporate** the water off. When the water evaporates from the salt solution, the salt is left behind.

Salt, like sugar, is made up of **crystals**. Each crystal is made up of millions of particles.

Salt is made of small crystals shaped like cubes.

Seawater stored in shallow pools evaporates in the Sun. The dissolved salts are used in the food industry.

4 Salt from salty water

Rana, Omar and Kavim are discussing how to get salt back from a salt solution.

a. Leave a saucer of salt solution near a radiator or on a sunny windowsill. You may need to leave it for a couple of days.

b. Explain what has happened when there is no further change.

WB 43

What do you think affects the size of salt crystals you get by evaporating water from a salt solution?

5 Which method gives the biggest salt crystals?

a. Will you get bigger salt crystals by evaporating the water off a salt solution quickly or slowly?

- Make a **prediction**.
- Can you give a reason?

b. Watch your teacher boil off the water from a salt solution. This will evaporate the water quickly.

Allow the salt and its container to cool down before looking at the crystals made.

Compare the salt crystals formed from this quick method with the salt crystals formed using the slow method in Activity 4. Use a magnifying glass.

- Which method gave the bigger crystals?
- Was your prediction correct?

WB 44

You looked at separating a solid from its solution. How can you separate two grainy solids that are mixed together if one is soluble in water and the other is not?

Separating sand and salt

6 Trouble in the kitchen

Look at the cartoon. Imagine you are Hiro's big brother or sister.

a. Write a plan, as a series of steps, to help your mother get her pure salt back. Show your plan to your teacher to check.

b. Try out the experiment in small groups. Your teacher can heat the solutions if required.

WB 45

Hint

Salt and sand grains are about the same size so sieving will not help. But salt is soluble in water whereas sand is not.

- What happens if you stir the sandy salt in water?
- How can you get rid of the undissolved sand?
- How can you get back the pure solid salt crystals?

Extension

Which is more soluble in water – salt or sugar?

Work in small groups.

a. Plan a fair test to answer this question. If you have time, try out your investigation.

b. Evaluate your method with another group.

- **How can you make your tests fairer?**
- **How can you improve the investigation to get more accurate results?**

WB 45

Checklist

Complete the checklist on page 46 in your Workbook.

- I can test whether materials are soluble or insoluble.
- I know how to separate a mixture of materials by sieving.
- I know how to separate a mixture of materials by filtering.
- I can describe how to collect a solid from a solution.

What have I learnt?

Answer these questions on the worksheet your teacher gives you.

1

a Name the changes of state of matter marked by letters A to D:

b Give the boiling point of water in °C.

c Give the melting point of ice in °C.

d Deena carefully holds a small mirror above a pan of boiling water. Describe and explain what she observes on the surface of the mirror.

2

Students were investigating the factors that might affect how quickly water evaporates.

One group decided to look at temperature.
They put one glass of water in their warm classroom and one in a cool shed outside.
They measured the water level every two days.

a Write down **two** things the group should keep the same to make it a fair test.

Here are the group's results:

Time in days	Height of water in classroom in mm	Height of water in shed in mm
0	65	65
2	61	64
4	57	62
6	53	62
8	47	60
10	44	58

b Draw two lines on the same graph to show their results.

c Where did the water evaporate more quickly, in the classroom or in the shed?

d Suggest what caused the difference between the two sets of results.

e What general pattern of results would you expect to see if you did more experiments to test your idea from part **d**?

3 **Look at the diagram below:**

- **a** What is the name of the process labelled A?
- **b** Describe how the water from the hills gets back to the sea.
- **c** Describe how clouds are formed. Include a change of state in your answer.

4 **An insoluble white solid is accidently mixed with a blue solid that does dissolve in water.**

- **a** Put the following actions in the correct order to get a pure sample of the blue solid back again. Use the letters **A** to **D**.
  - **A** Filter
  - **B** Leave in a warm place
  - **C** Add water
  - **D** Stir
- **b** Describe the purpose of each step in your answer to part **a**.

3 The life cycle of a flowering plant

In this unit, I am learning:

- that plants reproduce
- how seeds can be dispersed
- that insects pollinate some flowers
- that plants produce flowers, which have male and female parts
- that pollen from the male flower part fertilises the ovum (in the female flower part) to make a seed
- that flowering plants have a life cycle, which includes pollination, fertilisation, seed production, seed dispersal, and germination.

Keywords

fertilisation
flowers
germination
life cycle
plant
pollination
reproduce
reproduction
seeds

Why do you think **flowers** display their colourful petals?

1 What about seeds?

Work in pairs.

You know that **plants** grow from **seeds**. What do you already know about seeds? How are they made? Answer the questions in your Workbook and share your ideas with another pair.

Birds like eating seeds, and so do humans.

WB 49

Life cycles

Look at the photos of an apple tree flowering and fruiting. Flowering and fruiting are part of a plant's **life cycle**.

2 **What's inside an apple?**

Work in small groups.

Collect an apple and a kitchen knife.

a. Describe the apple in detail.

b.

- Cut the apple in half from top to bottom.
- Draw a labelled diagram of what you see inside.

c. Record how many seeds are inside the apple and describe them.

d. Find out the answers to these questions:

- Why does an apple tree grow blossom and fruit?
- Why do you think that the blossom and fruit appear at different times of the year?

WB 50

3.1 Monitoring plant growth

In this section, I am learning:

- how to monitor changes in plant growth over time
- how to record and display data over time.

Key words

discuss
evidenc
factors
fair tes
observe
presen
reproduce
reproduction
seedling
seeds
variables

Work with a partner. List the things you can observe or measure as they change on a growing plant.

Young plants are called seedlings

Growth and reproduction

All living things **reproduce** – this means that they create new individual offspring.

When flowering plants reproduce they make new flowering plants. These plants grow from **seeds** – you have observed plants growing. As you progress in science, you can add taking careful measurements to your observation skills.

Young plants that grow from seeds are called **seedlings**. Young plants grow into mature plants. Mature plants make seeds and the cycle of life begins again. You will look at plant life cycles in more detail in section 3.5.

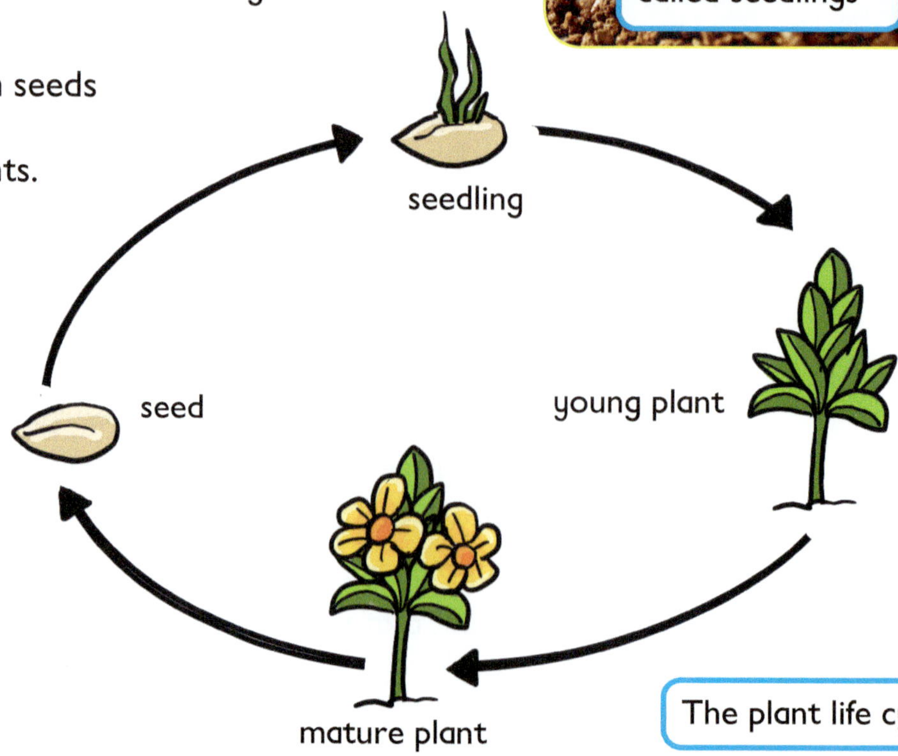

The plant life cycle

1 Observing plant growth

Work in small groups.

a. Choose one of these plants to grow from a seedling:

lettuce radish broad bean cress sunflower

b. Your teacher will show you the equipment and seeds you have to experiment with. **Discuss** these questions, then make a plan.

- How will you grow your seed or seedling?
- What does a seed or a seedling need to grow well?
- How will you make sure your seed or seedling gets what it needs?
- What do seedlings need that most seeds do not need?
- How will you **observe** and **present** your results to show the plant's growth? You must include some measurements.

Show your plan to your teacher before setting up the experiment.

c.

- Observe your plant over the next few weeks.
- Record your observations and measurements regularly. (You can review and evaluate your enquiry later in this unit.)

WB 51

Hint

Remember – you are responsible for the well-being of a living thing. Look after your plant well.

Measuring changes

Plants grow slowly over time. This makes it easier to take measurements. You can collect measured data very carefully. This will help you to get accurate results.

So, what kind of things can you measure as your plant grows?

You might choose to measure the height of a seedling – from the soil to its tip. To collect accurate **evidence**, you need to take each measurement in exactly the same way.

For example:

- make sure the zero line on your ruler lines up with the top of the soil
- gently hold the seedling straight up against the ruler's marked divisions
- get your eyes level with the tip of the seedling.
- read the length of the seedling to the nearest millimetre.

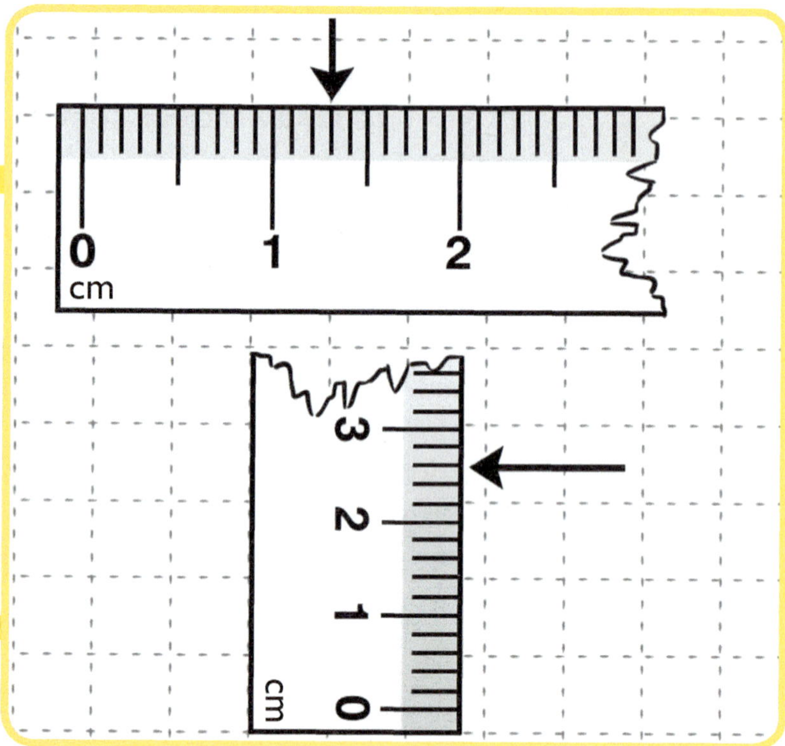

2 Making measurements

a. Besides the **height** of a plant, what other measurements can you take using a ruler?

b. Read these two measurements and record them in your Workbook.

WB 52

Recording observations and measurements

You can record your observations as the plant grows by:

- drawing pictures
- taking digital images at regular intervals.

You can record your measurements in a table with headings like this:

Time in days	Height in mm

When you finish monitoring your plant, you can present your results on a line graph (because the **variables** on both axes are measured in numbers).

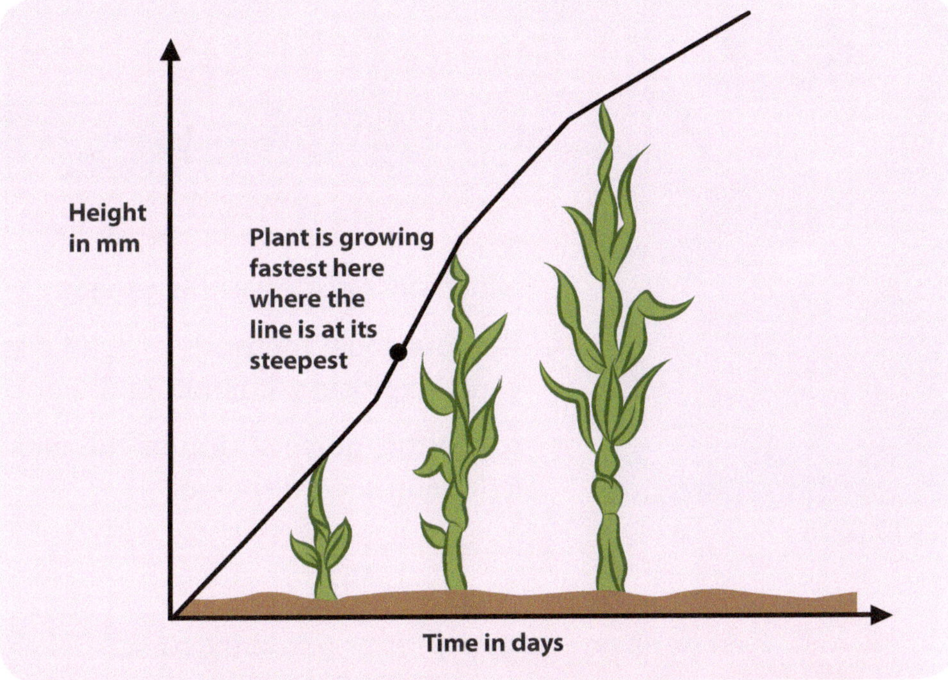

You have taken measurements with a ruler. What other observations can you make as your plant grows?

Extension

A group investigates four different plant seedlings, each from a different type of plant, to see which grows the fastest in one week.

a. Which variables (factors) need to be controlled to make it a fair test?

b. Which type of graph can they display their results on – a bar chart or a line graph?

Explain why.

WB 53

Checklist

Complete the checklist on page 53 in your Workbook.

- I can observe and measure changes in plant growth over time.
- I know how to record and display data about plant growth over time.

3.2 Seed dispersal

In this section, I am learning:

- why plants disperse their seeds
- the four main methods of seed dispersal: wind, explosion, animals and water
- to identify germination as the process following seed dispersal.

Keywords

animal, dispersal, explosion, fruit, germination, interpret (findings), predict, test, variable, water, wind

Remember – many plants grow from seeds. Young plants can sometimes be found growing some distance away from the parent plant. How did they get there?

1 Numbers of seeds

On page 49 you looked at the inside of an apple. How many seeds did the apple contain?

Your teacher will give you another **fruit** to look at, such as a strawberry. A strawberry has its seeds on the outside.

a. Why do you think so many fruits contain far more than one seed?

b. Discuss your ideas in a small group and write them in your Workbook.

WB 54

Space to grow

Plants do not grow well if they are crowded together. They need some space around them. If the plants are too crowded, they might not get enough of the things they need to grow well.

Seed dispersal

After a plant's seeds have developed, they need to be spread around to give them a better chance of growing into healthy new plants. Plants spread (**disperse**) their seeds in different ways.

1. Seed dispersal by wind

Some plants' seeds get blown a distance from the parent plant by the **wind**.
For example, dandelions make very light seeds that are attached to their own tiny parachutes. These parachutes carry the seeds high into the sky.

Maple trees also use the wind to disperse their seeds. These seeds have 'helicopter' wings and spin around rapidly when they fall from the tree – like the blades on a helicopter. The wings catch the wind and allow the seeds to travel a distance from the tree.

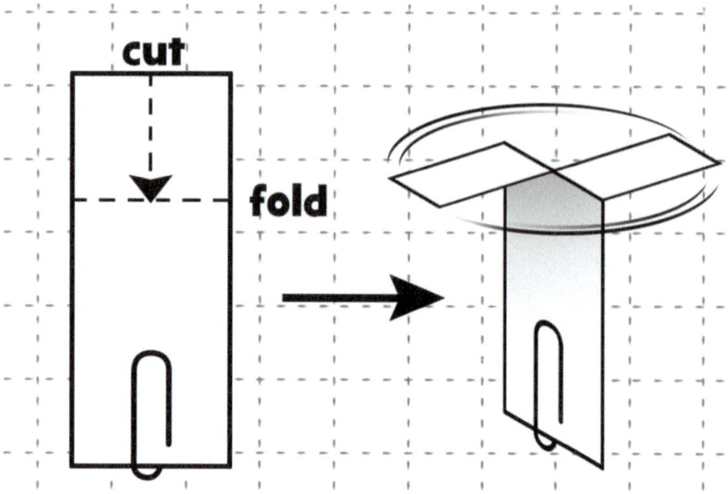

You can model a maple seed by making a paper 'spinner' as shown in the picture.

2 'Helicopter seeds' investigation

Work in pairs.

a. Choose one of the ideas in the picture to investigate.

b. Make a **prediction** and explain it.

- What **variable** will you change in each **test**?
- What will you measure to judge the effect of changing your chosen variable?
- What variables will you keep the same in each test to make your investigation fair?

c. Plan a method and show your teacher.

- Do you think it will be a good idea to repeat each test?
- Why do you think this?

d. Carry out your investigation and record your results in your Workbook.

e. Look carefully at your results.

- How will you **interpret** your findings?
- What conclusions can you draw after your investigation?
- How can you improve your investigation?

WB 54

2. Seed dispersal by explosion

Some seeds inside the fruit of a plant are spread when the fruit bursts open. This is called dispersal by **explosion**. The seeds grow inside the fruit, which dries up when the seeds are ready to release. On a hot day, the air inside the fruit expands and the outer casing suddenly splits apart. The seeds shoot out in all directions.

Gorse and sweet peas spread their seeds by explosion

3. Seed dispersal by animals

Many animals, including birds, feed on seeds from plants, or on the fruit the plants produce (which contains the seeds). The seeds often have tough coatings. They pass through the animal undamaged and are deposited in their solid waste.

In this way, the seed is transported by the **animal**, from the place where it is eaten to the place where the animal deposits the seed. The seed is mixed in with the animal's solid waste. Solid waste is rich in nutrients – this will help the new plant to grow well. Date and fig seeds are spread in this way.

Interesting fact

Rodents damage seeds by chewing them but birds swallow seeds whole. Scientists think that the hot taste of a chilli plant puts off rodents but not birds. The seeds eaten by birds are deposited largely unharmed, so they have a good chance of growing into new chilli plants.

Some seeds are sticky or grow in fruits that stick to the fur of animals as they brush past the plant. These seeds often have hooks or spikes on their outer casing. The seeds fall off the animal some time, and some distance, later.

All sorts of animals eat seeds and fruit containing seeds. Birds feeding on berries can deposit the seeds many miles from the parent bush.

Burdock has hooks growing on its fruit. These get tangled in animal fur.

4. Seed dispersal by water

Some plants use **water** to carry their seeds to different places. Willow trees often grow near streams or rivers – their light, fluffy seeds can float on the water (or in the wind).

Some plants that grow near the sea have tough, woody seed shells, for example, coconuts. These can survive for a long time in water and float thousands of kilometres across oceans before meeting dry land again.

Once a plant's seeds have been dispersed, the seeds start to grow into a new plant. This is called **germination**. You will find out more about germination in Unit 4.

Interesting fact

The largest seed in the world is the double coconut from the coco-de-mer palm tree. It can measure up to 50 cm right around and can have a mass of up to 18 kg.

Extension

Think about coconuts.

a. Which features of a coconut make it capable of growing so far away from the parent tree?

b. Where do the new shoots and roots start growing from in a coconut?

c. What do you see inside a coconut when you crack open its shell? Can you explain your observations?

WB 56

Checklist

Complete the checklist on page 56 in your Workbook.

- I can explain why plants disperse their seeds.
- I can explain four main methods of seed dispersal: wind, explosion, animals, and water.
- I can identify germination as the process that follows seed dispersal.

3.3 The parts of a flower

Keywords

carpel
female
flowers
insects
male
petal
pollen
reproduce
reproduction
sepal
stamen

In this section, I am learning:

- that plants produce flowers, which have male and female organs
- the main parts of a flower
- the functions of the main parts of a flower.

Flowers come in many different shapes, colours and sizes. Have you ever noticed that despite their differences they have a lot of structures in common?

Flowering plants have **flowers** so that the plant can **reproduce**. Each flower has **male** organs and **female** organs. This diagram shows the general structure of the parts of a flowering plant.

Each type of flowering plant will produce variations of this structure but all the parts needed for **reproduction** will be there.

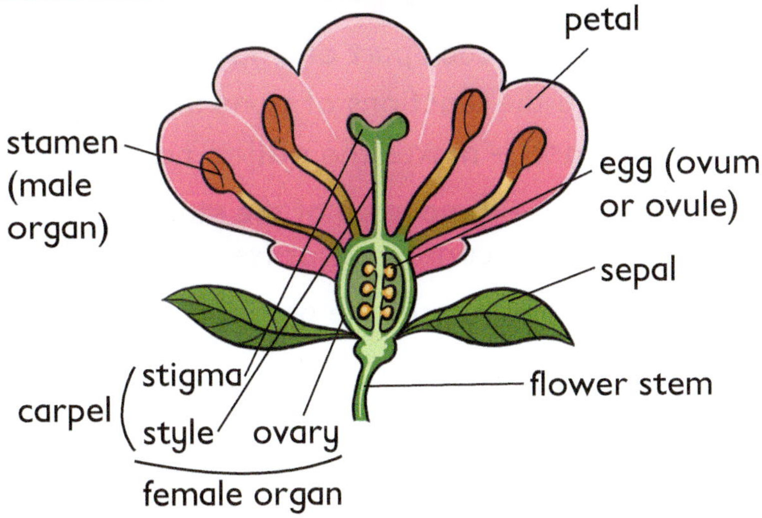

1 Matching the parts of a real flower

Your teacher will give you a flower to look at.

You can compare this with the general flower in the diagram.

a. Draw a sketch to identify:

- a **petal**
- a **sepal**
- a **stamen**
- a **carpel**.

b. Show your sketch and flower to another pair. Do they agree with your labels? Do you agree with theirs?

WB 57

2 **Making a model flower**

Work in pairs.

a. Look at a flower in detail using a hand lens.

b. Use paper, card, pipe cleaners and buttons (plus any other things you can think of) to make a model of a simple flower. Make sure your model shows the different parts of a flower.

c. Place your completed flower in a vase with other flowers from your class to make a flower display.

d. Answer these questions in your Workbook:

- In what ways are these model flowers different to each other?
- Is there another model that is very similar to yours? Can you describe how?

WB 57

What each part of the flower does

The job that each part of a flower does is called its function.

Here are the functions of some important parts of a flower:

- **stamen** – makes the **pollen** needed for reproduction (see section 3.4).
- **carpel** – is made up of the stigma, style and ovary. The stigma accepts pollen and the ovary contains eggs (see section 3.4).
- **sepals** – protect the petals in the buds.
- **petals** – attract **insects**.

Extension

Look at the diagram of the general structure of a flower on page 59.

Try to learn this and the functions of each part listed above.

Now close your book.

a. In your Workbook, draw the general structure of a flower.

b. Swap your diagram with a partner and open your books again.

c. Correct your partner's diagram if necessary.

WB 57

3.4 Pollination and fertilisation

In this section, I am learning:

- to identify pollination as the next stage after germination
- how insects pollinate some flowers
- how seeds are formed.

Keywords
female
fertilisation
flowers
fruit
insects
ovum
pollen
pollination
reproduce
reproduction
seed production

Have you noticed the yellow or orange dust you get on your fingers when you handle some **flowers**? This is made up of **pollen** grains.

Do you know why plants have pollen grains?

1 Why do plants make pollen?

These friends are sitting in a wild flower meadow.

They notice **insects** landing on the flowers and wonder why.

Work in small groups.

a. Whose ideas do you agree with?

b. Why do you think insects regularly visit flowers?

c. Write a summary of your ideas in your Workbook.

WB 58

Where is pollen made in a flowering plant?

Flowering plants make pollen in the male part of the flower. This is called the stamen. The pollen can be collected from the top of the stamen.

Like all living things, flowering plants need to **reproduce**. To make a new plant, pollen from one plant needs to be transferred to another plant of the same species. This is where insects can be useful.

When insects, such as bees, land on a flower the pollen grains stick to the insect's body.

When the insect visits another flower, the pollen rubs off and sticks to the **female** part of another plant. This part is called the carpel. The carpel is right in the middle of the flower – see page 59.

You can see the stamens with their orange pollen grains around the centre (carpel) of this lily flower.

The process of transferring pollen is called **pollination**.

Insects, such as bees, pollinate flowers.

Extension

a. What do you know about hay fever? Make some notes.

b. Use your notes to produce a booklet about hay fever for people to read in a doctor's waiting room.

WB 58

How do flowering plants attract insects?

Flowering plants need insects to transfer their pollen. They have brightly coloured petals to attract the insects' attention. Insects can also smell the sweet, sugary nectar that flowering plants produce. The nectar is like a reward for the insects that visit the plant.

The nectar is deep inside the flower. To feed on the nectar, the insect must brush past the stamen. This means the insect gets showered in pollen grains!

An ant gets covered in pollen as it feeds on nectar at the bottom of the flower.

A butterfly feeding on nectar.

A bat helping to transfer pollen grains.

Interesting fact

It's not just insects that feed on nectar and help pollination. Bats, hummingbirds and other small mammals also feed on nectar and can transfer pollen from one flower to another.

2 Acting out pollination

Work in groups of five or six.

Plan a presentation of what happens in the process of pollination.

You can either:

- act out pollination as it actually happens in nature
- or make up your own story to model pollination.

WB 58

Fertilisation

Remember – for many plants, insects transfer the pollen from one plant to another.

- The pollen comes from the male organ of the flower, called the stamen. When they leave a flower, insects have pollen stuck to their legs and bodies.
- When the insect arrives at another flower to feed on its nectar, it pushes past the carpel, the female organ. The carpel has a sticky pad at its top (called the stigma) to gather pollen from the insect's body.

The female part of the flower (carpel) with pollen from a male part (stamen) about to fertilise an egg cell (**ovum**).

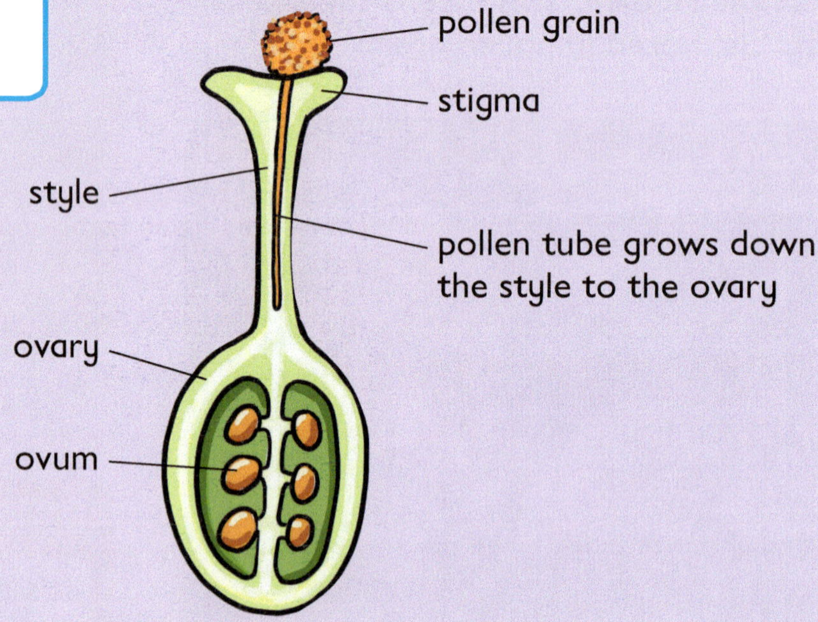

Fertilisation results in **seed production**, as the **ovum** develops into a seed inside the ovary.

The ovary changes into a **fruit** to help the seeds to disperse. This will improve the seed's chances of developing into a healthy new plant, because it will not have to compete with the parent plant for water, light and nutrients.

To summarise:

- The process where pollen is transferred is called pollination.
- The process where the pollen fertilises the female egg (ovum) is called fertilisation.

Pollination has to happen first and then fertilisation occurs.

3 Modelling the story of pollination and fertilisation

Use your flower models from page 60 to show how pollination and then fertilisation take place in a flowering plant.
You will need to cut out a bee-shaped piece of card to use in the pollination stage.
Describe your presentation in your Workbook.
Your teacher may choose one group to give their presentation to the rest of the class.

WB 59

4 Fieldwork

Work in small groups.

a. Walk around your school grounds or a local park to look for plants that:

- have been fertilised (and so are fruiting)
- are dispersing seeds
- are in bloom to attract pollinating insects.

b. Make a note of your observations in your Workbook.

WB 59

Extension

Work in pairs.

a. What makes each part of a flower most effective in carrying out its job? Design the perfect flower on a poster.

b. Write labels to explain why each feature is effective.

c. Display your poster for the rest of the class to see.

WB 60

Checklist

Complete the checklist on page 60 in your Workbook.

- I know that plants produce flowers that have male and female organs.
- I can label the main parts of a flower.
- I know what the main parts of a flower do.
- I can identify pollination as the next stage after germination.
- I can describe how insects pollinate some flowers.
- I know how seeds are formed.

3.5 Life cycles of flowering plants

In this section, I am learning:

- that flowering plants have a life cycle
- that their life cycle includes pollination, fertilisation, seed production, seed dispersal, and germination.

Key words

growth
life cycle
reproduce
reproduction

The cycle of life

All living things have a **life cycle**. This includes stages of **growth** and always involves a form of **reproduction** (making new individuals).

You have just been thinking about the human life cycle. We start life as babies, then grow into children, then youths. When we become adults, we may have our own children. We then become elderly before finally we die.

Think of the youngest person in your family and the oldest person.

Discuss with a partner at which age:

- **babies become children**
- **children become youths**
- **youths become adults**
- **adults become elderly.**

Flowering plants, like all living things, also have a life cycle. The main stages of the life cycle of a flowering plant are the growth of:

- a seed into a seedling
- a seedling into a young plant
- a young plant into a mature plant (which starts the cycle all over again by making new seeds).

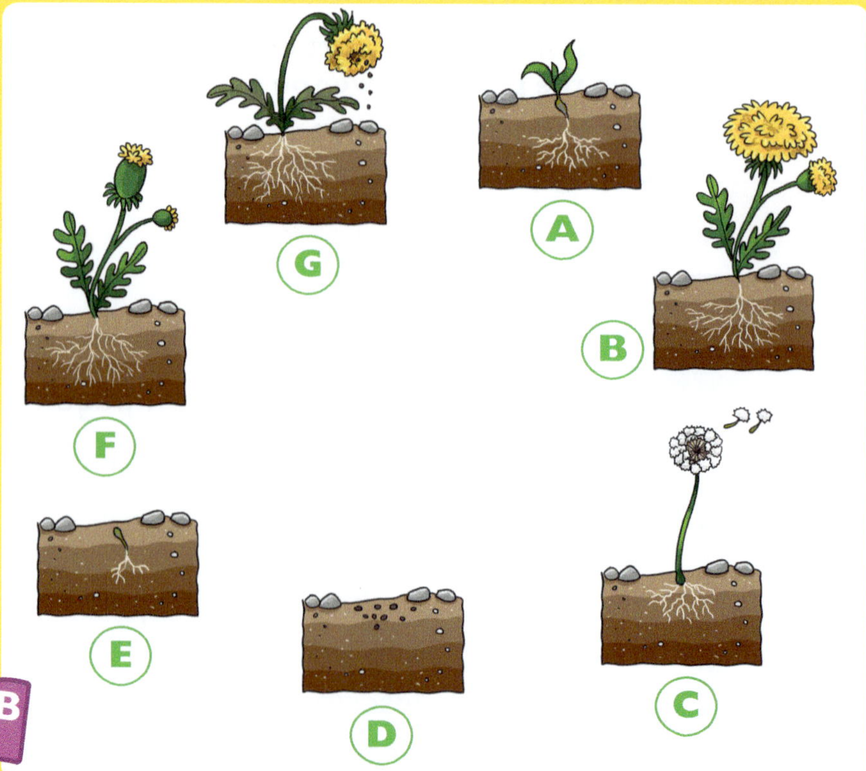

I Arrange a life cycle

Sort the pictures into the circular life cycle of a flower.

WB 61

The life cycle of a flowering plant

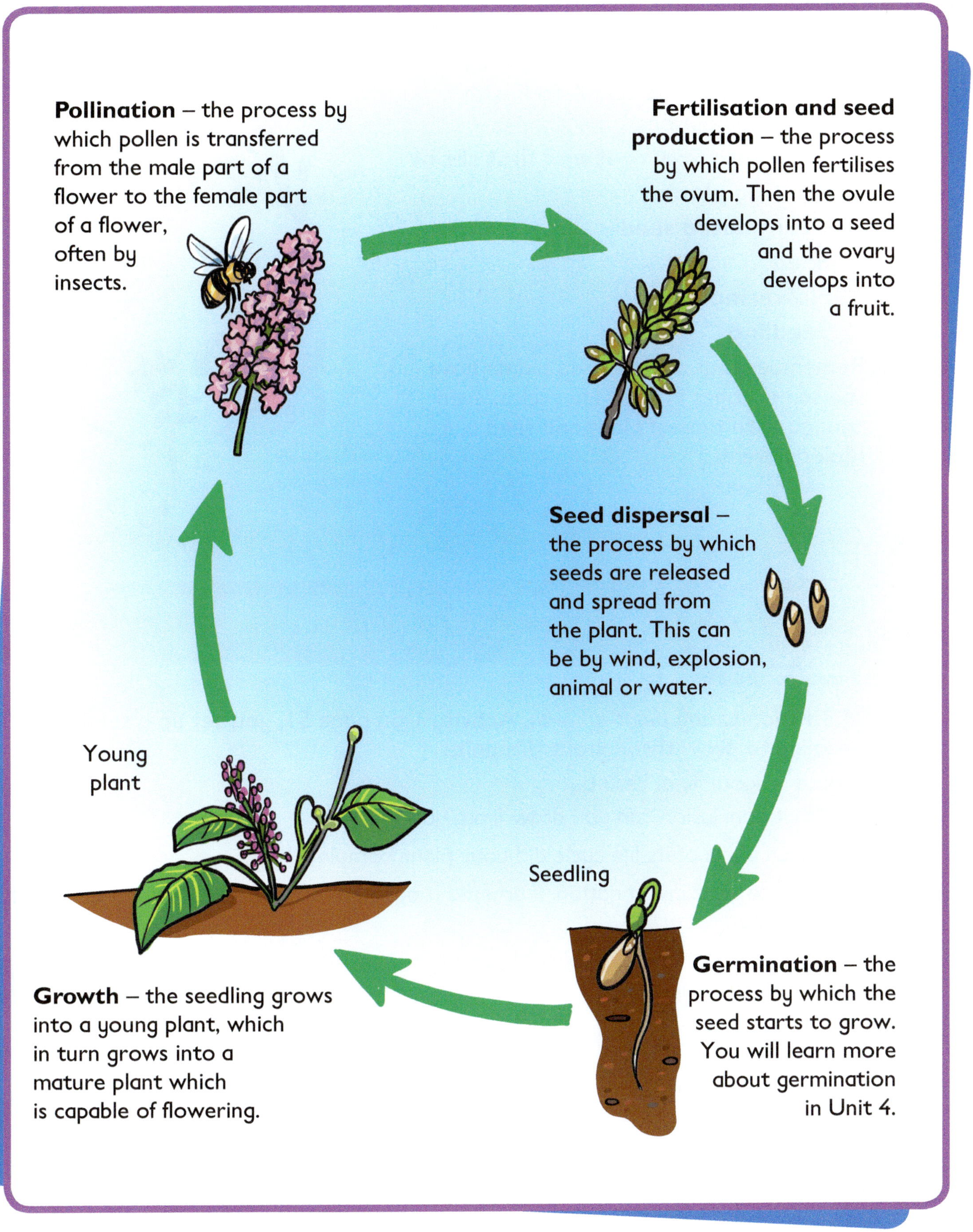

2 Label parts of a life cycle

Here is another version of the flowering plant life cycle. It is missing all its labels.

Without looking back at the life cycle on page 67 match letters A to F with the following options:

- **Seed with first root and first shoot**
- **Fruiting plant**
- **Germinated seed**
- **Seed**
- **Flowering plant**
- **Seedling**

Remember that all flowering plants have the same stages in their life cycles, even though each type of plant and seed can look different.

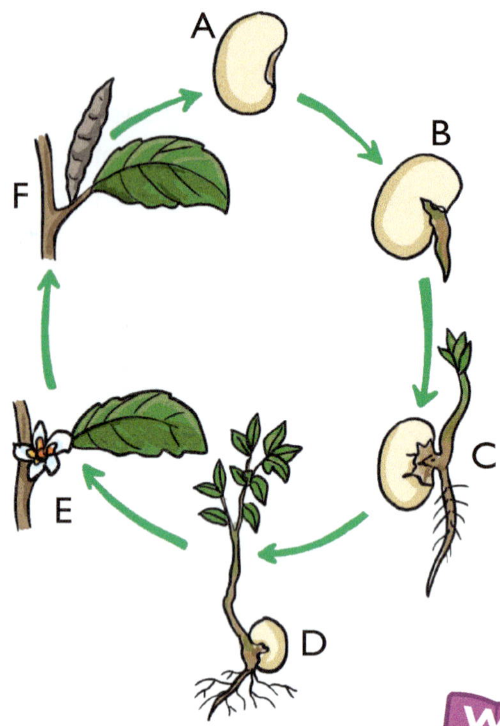

WB 61

3 Final report

In 3.1 *Monitoring plant growth*, Activity 1 on page 51, you set up a seed or seedling to grow throughout this unit.

Write up your final results.

a. What conclusion can you draw from your results?

b. Which parts of its life cycle did your plant complete?

c. Evaluate your investigation. If you did it again, would you do anything differently? Explain why.

WB 62

Extension

Mrs Edwards and Mrs Ricci each grow poppies.

Mrs Edwards cuts her flowers and brings them indoors to make a nice display.

Mrs Ricci likes to leave her flowers blooming in the garden.

After five years, Mrs Ricci has many more poppies in her garden than Mrs Edwards.

Can you explain why?

WB 62

Checklist

Complete the checklist on page 63 in your Workbook.

- I know that flowering plants have a life cycle.
- I know that their life cycle includes pollination, fertilisation, seed production, seed dispersal, and germination.
- I can construct the life cycle of a flowering plant.

What have I learnt?

Answer these questions on the worksheet your teacher gives you.

1 Name the part of a plant that:

a protects the petals

b holds up the flower

c is usually brightly coloured

d keeps (anchors) it in one place

e contains the seeds.

2 Solve the anagrams below:

a The process in which pollen gets from one plant to another.

l P l i t n o o a n i

b The process in which a seed is first produced.

e r i F i s i t o t n l a

c The process in which a seed forms a root and shoot and starts growing.

m e n i t G i n a o r

3 **a** What do we mean by 'seed dispersal'?

b Match each seed (letters A to D) with the way it is dispersed (numbers 1 to 4).

A

B

C

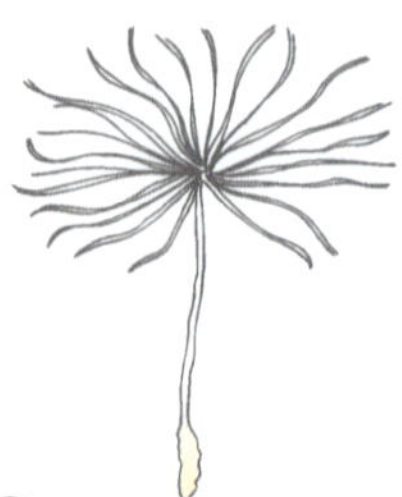

D

1 **wind**

2 **animals eating them**

3 **explosion**

4 **animals, stuck to their fur**

4 Look at the inside of a flower drawn below.

a Choose words from this box to label the flower:

sepal	ovary	stigma
stamen	petal	style

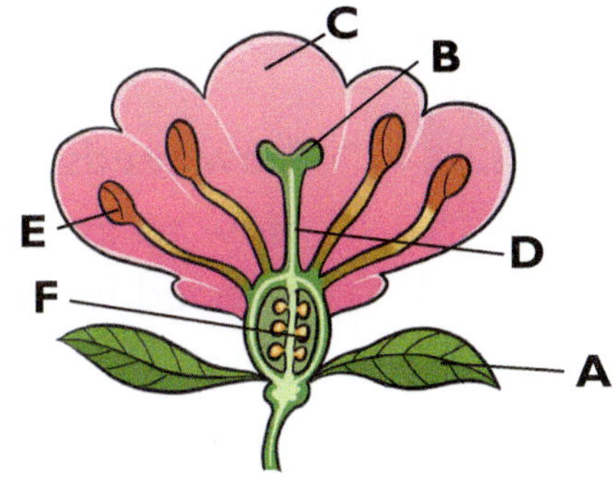

Choose words from part a) to answer the questions in b) below:

b Which part of the flower:

i makes pollen grains?

ii develops into a fruit?

iii do pollen grains from another plant stick to?

c Name two insects that carry pollen from one plant to another.

5 Look at this life cycle of a flowering plant:

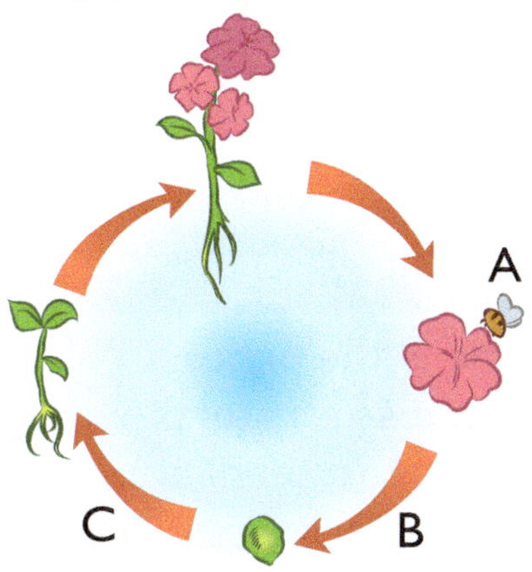

a Name the processes shown by letters A, B and C in the life cycle.

b Where is the seed formed in a flowering plant? Choose the correct letter:

A in the stamen

B in the ovary

C in the style

D on the stigma

c Why do you think that many plants produce lots of seeds?

4 Investigating plant growth

In this unit, I am learning:

- how seeds germinate
- how to investigate the conditions needed for seeds to germinate
- what plants need to grow well
- how to investigate the conditions needed for plants to grow well.

Key words

germinate
germination
plant
seed

Why do you think that most seeds germinate in springtime? Why do farmers and gardeners use greenhouses to grow plants?

Part of a plant's life cycle is the process of **germination** – when a **seed** starts to grow into a young **plant** (a seedling).

Here is a scientific diagram of the inside of a seed, cut lengthways:

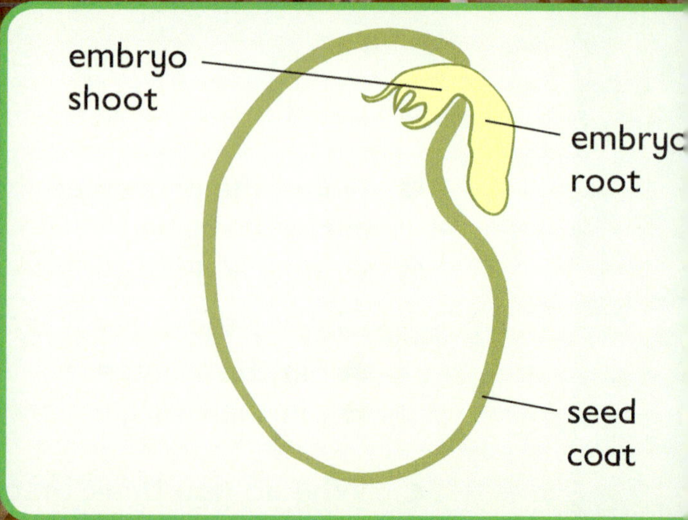

The structure of a bean seed

What conditions do seeds need to germinate? What affects the plants they grow into?

Acorns grow into large oak trees.

1 **More about seeds**

Work in small groups.

Discuss the following questions.

a. Which usually grows first, the embryo root or the shoot? Suggest why.

b. Why do seeds usually contain food stores?

c. Which way will the root grow in the soil?

d. Does it matter which way up a seed is planted?

Write some notes in your Workbook.

WB 65

4.1 What makes seeds germinate?

In this section, I am learning:

how to investigate what makes seeds germinate by:

- planning an investigation
- carrying out my investigation and drawing conclusions from its results
- evaluating my investigation into germination.

Key words

conclusion
evaluate
factor
germinate
germination
seeds

Look at the germination of the seed as it turns into a seedling:

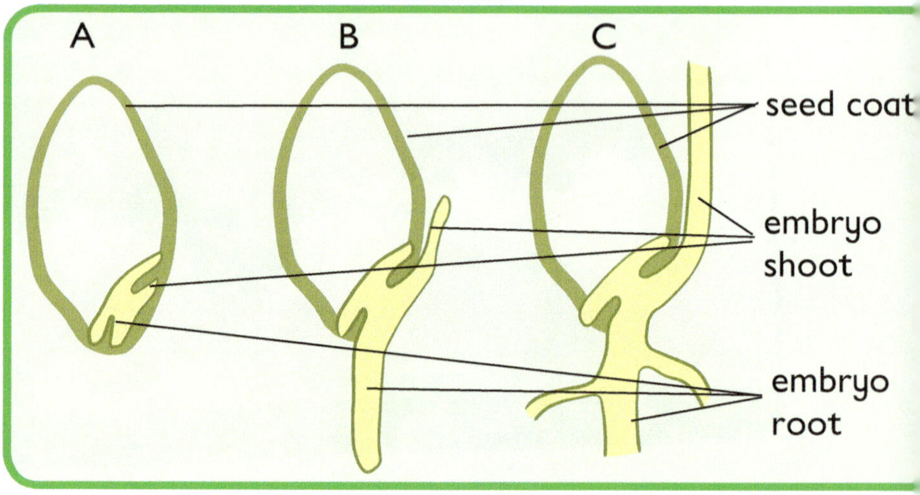

How do scientists know what seeds need to germinate?

In this section you will investigate the conditions that **seeds** need to **germinate**.

Look at this investigation a group carried out to see if air was needed for a seed to germinate.

Finding out if a seed needs air to germinate

Darya explains what her group did.

1 Do seeds need air to germinate?

Here are the group's results from the experiment Darya described:

Factor that was changed	Number of seeds germinated
With air in bag	16
No air in bag	5

a. Suggest a **conclusion** for this investigation and record it in your Workbook.

b. Discuss the two questions below with a partner:

- Why did the group use 20 seeds in each dish and not just one seed?
- The group left the dishes in the same place for two days. Which **factors** did this control?

WB 66

Extension

Evaluate Darya's group's investigation. Why did a few seeds germinate in the bag that the group said had 'no air' in it?

WB 66

Interesting fact

In frozen soil in Siberia, scientists found fruit that was more than 30 000 years old! They extracted the parts that seeds grow from, treated them, and managed to grow plants and even produce flowers.

4.2 Doing your own investigation into germination

Keywords

conclusion, factor, fair test, germinate, germination, line graph, measure, observe, predict/prediction, record, reliable, variable, warmth, water

In this section, I am learning:

- how to investigate the germination of seeds further, making many of the decisions myself
- how to make a prediction about germination using my scientific knowledge

Fair testing

To carry out this type of investigation, you need to set up a "**fair test**".

- In a fair test, you choose one **factor** (or **variable**) to investigate.
- You then vary this factor and **measure** or **observe** what effect this has.
- All the other factors that might matter are kept the same.

In investigations involving living things, fair testing can be tricky. This is because all living things are different, even in the same species.

Some seeds have a fault – they will not germinate no matter what you do. What can scientists do to solve this?

When scientists investigate seeds they will use many of them:

- They use plenty of the same type of seeds when investigating one type of seed.
- To see if their **conclusions** apply to all seeds in general, they will test many different types of seeds.

This makes their results more **reliable**.

Why should these students use more than one seed? Can you really trust the results if you test just one seed?

Kaden and his friends have some ideas about what affects **germination**.

1 Which factors do you think might affect germination?

Work as a small group.

How many factors can you think of that might affect the germination of a seed?

(You do not know if they will or not until you test them – that includes Kaden's and his friends' ideas.)

- Choose one person to list all the factors on a piece of paper.
- Discuss the list – are there any ideas you don't agree on?
- Make a final list of factors in your Workbook.

WB 67

Investigating the effect of water on germination

You can investigate any one of the factors you thought of in Activity 1.

Was **water** one of the factors you listed?

This is the factor you will investigate first.

A good investigation starts with a good question. We often use this question as the title of the investigation when writing it up.

Here is your question to investigate:

Do seeds need water to germinate?

When you investigate a question, you often make a **prediction**. A good prediction is supported by a reason for the prediction.

2 Making a prediction

You have experimented with seeds. You know about their structures. You have seen what happens to them when seeds germinate.

Make a prediction about the effect of water on germination.

Explain your reasoning.

WB 67

3 Planning your investigation

Use these questions to help you plan your germination investigation. Write your answers in your Workbook.

a. What are you trying to find out?

b. What will you change in each test to find the answer?

c. What will you observe to judge the effect of water on germination?

d. What will you keep the same to make it a fair test?

e. How will you carry out your investigation? What equipment will you need?

f. How many seeds will you need to test?

g. Is your plan safe?

Safety: Remember to wash your hands after handling seeds or compost. Ask your teacher to check your finished plan.

WB 68

4 Completing your investigation

a. Set up your dishes and seeds. Check them after two or three days.

What happened to the seeds? Write your observations in your Workbook.

b. What is your conclusion?

c. What type of seed did you use? Can you be sure your conclusion applies to all types of seed?

d. How can you make your results more reliable?

WB 70

Extension

Isabella has an idea about water and germination. She says, "I think that the more water you add to seeds, the faster they germinate."

a. How can you change your plan in Activity 3 to test Isabella's idea?

b. What do you think will happen? Sketch a line graph in your Workbook.

c. Why did you choose that shape of line on your sketch graph? Explain your answer.

WB 71

Hint

In a sketch graph you do not need to put a scale on the graph – the line you draw just shows a rough pattern.

Interesting fact

Seed banks are places where seeds are kept in long-term storage. The seeds are stored in conditions that stop germination from taking place without damaging the seeds. We store the seeds to stop some rare species of plant from becoming extinct.

The effect of light and temperature on germination

You completed an investigation about germination and water. You discovered that seeds will not germinate without water – so you must use water in all your other seed investigations.

Now you are going to look at the effect of light and temperature on seed germination.

These two children are discussing germination.

You do not want seeds to germinate in their packets before you plant them. So, dried (or 'desiccated') seeds are stored in packets.

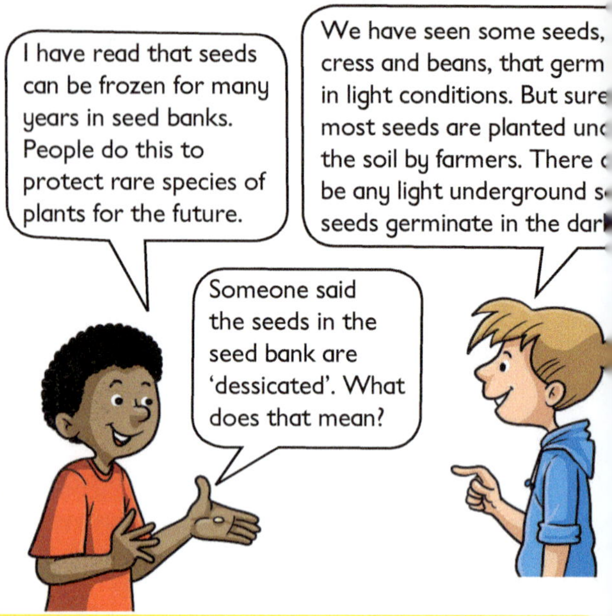

5 Investigating the effect of light and temperature on germination

Work in small groups.

a. In your Workbook, write your predictions:

- How do you think light or dark affects the germination of seeds?
- Do you think seeds germinate better in warm or cold conditions?

b. Carry out your investigation.

- Some groups can investigate the effect of light or dark in cold conditions and some in warm conditions.
- Some groups can investigate the effect of warm or cold temperatures in light conditions and some in dark conditions.

After two or three days, share your results with the other groups' results.

Record all the results in a table in your Workbook.

c. Draw a bar chart to show the class results.

d. What did you learn from your results? Write your conclusion in your Workbook.

Hint

Keep some of the seedlings that grew well. You will investigate them in section 4.3.

Hint

You draw a bar chart when the factor (or variable) you change in each test is described by words, such as "cold" or "dark".

WB 72

Extension

How can you improve the class investigation into the effect of light and temperature on germination?

Think about:

- **fair testing – in a fair test you choose one factor (or variable) to investigate. This factor changes but all the other factors that might have an effect, must stay the same. Did you manage to control all the other factors?**
- **reliability – did you test enough seeds to trust your conclusions?**

Hint

You only looked at one type of seed. Can you be sure that the conclusions are true for all types of seed?

WB 74

Summary

As you have discovered, the conditions needed for seeds to germinate are:

- **water**
- **warmth**
- **air.**

Usually seeds can germinate in the dark (beneath the soil), but some types of seed do need light to start germination.

Checklist

Complete the checklist on page 74 in your Workbook.

- I can plan an investigation into the germination of seeds.
- I can make a prediction about germination using my scientific knowledge.
- I can carry out an investigation about germination and draw conclusions from the results.
- I can evaluate an investigation into germination.

4.3 Investigating plant growth

In this section, I am learning:

- what green plants need to grow
- how to investigate different factors in plant growth.

Key words

growth
measure
record
present results
variable

How can we monitor the growth of a plant?

In section 3.1, you saw how we can monitor the **growth** of plants over time. Without looking back, discuss with a partner the different ways of observing or measuring how well a plant grows over time.

Look at the children sharing ideas about how plants grow:

Hint

What can you count as time passes?
What can you **measure**?
What equipment, including measuring instruments, do you need to monitor a seedling's growth?

1 **What are your ideas about how plants grow?**

Work in small groups.

a. Discuss the ideas in the picture. You can make notes in your Workbook.

b. On a large piece of paper, write a speech bubble that summarises your own group's thoughts on how plants grow.

Display your speech bubble for the rest of the class to see.

WB 75

Presenting your results

Scientists often use tables to **record** data from investigations. Design your table **before** carrying out your investigation. Then you can record the **results** in your table **as you collect the data**.

Numerical data can be **presented** on graphs – this helps you to see patterns in your data.

Scientists usually follow a set routine when they:

- write headings in tables
- label the axes on graphs.

If you investigate the effect of temperature on plant growth:

- the **variable you will change** is the temperature – you can try growing a plant in "very cold", "cold", "warm", "hot" and "very hot" places
- the variable **you will measure** could be the height of a seedling, after three days.

In this case, draw your table and label your graph as shown here.

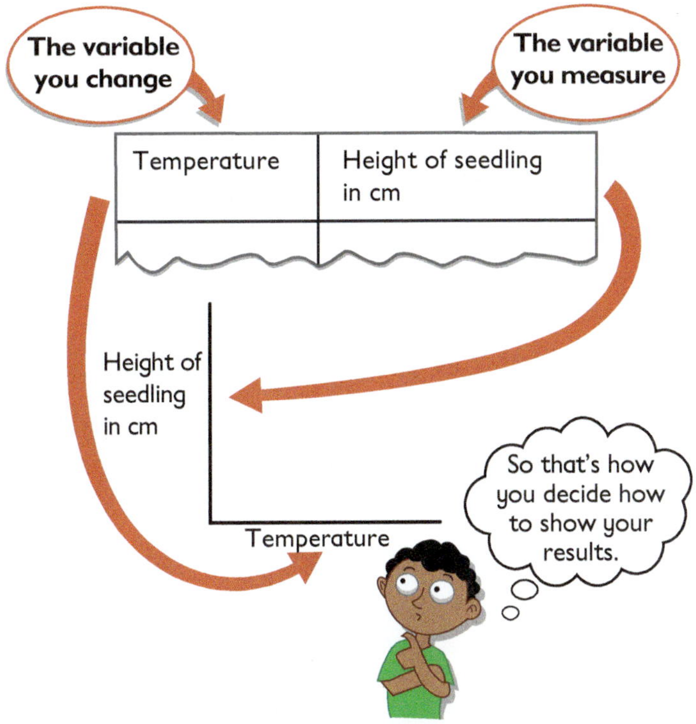

There is one more thing for you to decide. **Do you draw a bar chart or a line graph?**

- If the variable you change (the one in the first column of your table) is described by words, draw a bar chart.
- If the variable you change is measured or counted, and described using numbers, draw a line graph.

2 Graph decisions

Work in pairs.

In the example above, temperature is shown along the bottom of the graph. If you describe the temperature as "very cold", "cold", "warm", "hot" and "very hot", draw a bar chart.

Discuss the following questions and write your answers in your Workbook.

a. How many bars do you need to draw?

b. What do you have to do in your investigation to display your results on a line graph?

WB 75

4.4 Energy for plant growth

In this section, I am learning:

- that plants get energy from light to grow

Keywords

conclusion
control
energy
evaluate
growth
light energy
measure
present
water

How plants get energy

All living things, including plants, need **energy** to stay alive. They get their energy from their food. Animals need to eat plants or other animals to get their energy. But plants are lucky – they can make their own food!

To make their food, plants need:

- carbon dioxide gas from the air
- **water** from the soil and
- **light energy** from the Sun.

Plants use their green parts as 'mini-factories' to make food. These are mainly found in their leaves. The leaves absorb carbon dioxide gas and get water from the roots.

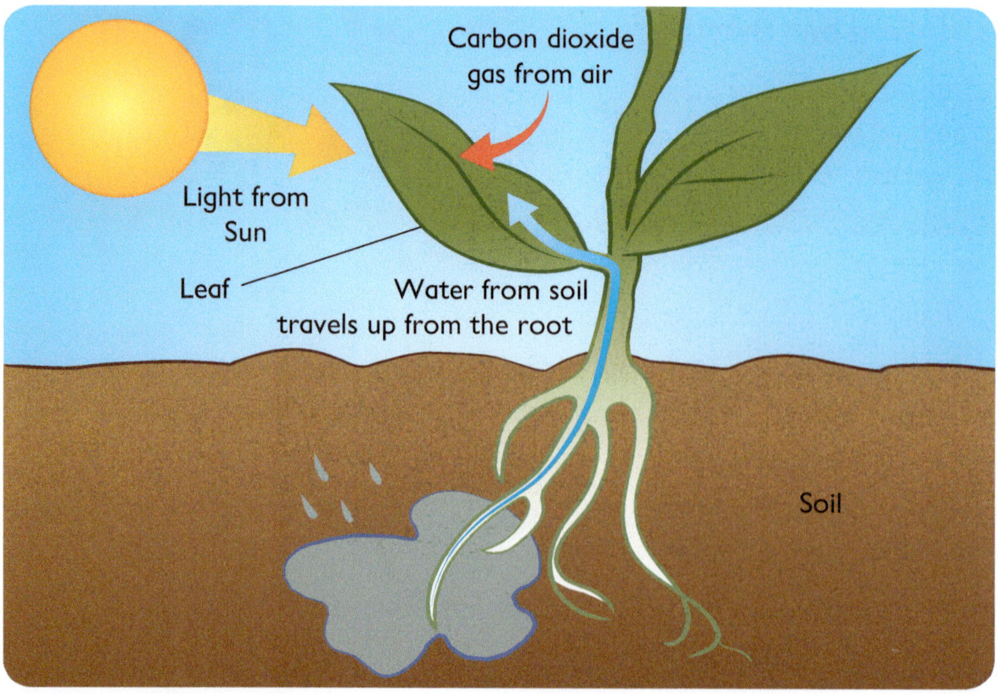

Plants need carbon dioxide gas, water and light to grow well.

Energy from sunlight helps carbon dioxide and water react together to make sugar. This is plant food.

The plant's energy is stored in the sugar, and the starch it can make, ready for use where and when it is needed.

Looking at light and plant growth

In Stage 3 you observed what happened when a green plant was left in a dark cupboard. What did the plant look like when you took it out of the cupboard? Look at the photo below:

The runner bean plant on the left was grown in normal light conditions. The plant on the right was grown in the dark. All other factors were the same. Notice that although the plant grown in the dark is taller, it does not look as healthy as the plant grown in the light.

Scientists do not just grow plants in the dark to see if light is needed for healthy growth. They set up a **control** experiment.

In the control experiment, plants are treated exactly the same as the ones in the dark. The only difference is that they are given normal light conditions. This means it can only be the level of light that causes any differences in **growth**.

In Activity 1, you can monitor the growth of seedlings. You will take **measurements** now, as well as observing changes over time.

1 **How can we show that green plants need light energy for growth?**

Work in small groups.

In this investigation, try to make as many decisions as you can.

a. What plants will you use? (You can use the cress seedlings from the previous section.)

b. How will you monitor the growth of the seedlings regularly over time in light and dark?

c. Design a table to record your measurements and observations each time you check the seedlings.

d. **Present** both sets of your measurements on the same graph.

e. What evidence did you use to make your **conclusion** about the best conditions for growing a green plant? Explain your answer.

f. **Evaluate** your investigation.

WB 76

Checklist

Complete the checklist on page 77 in your Workbook.

- I know what green plants need to grow.
- I can plan an investigation into a factor (such as light) that affects plant growth.
- I can carry out my investigation into plant growth and draw a graph to display the results.
- I can draw conclusions and evaluate my investigation into plant growth.

What have I learnt?

Answer these questions on the worksheet your teacher gives you.

1 **a** Which of the seeds in the table below will germinate?

Copy the table and fill in the last column with "yes" or "no".

Seeds	Conditions	Will the seed germinate?
A	Very cold, no water, light	
B	Very cold, no water, dark	
C	Very cold, water, light	
D	Very cold, water, dark	
E	Warm, water, light	
F	Warm, water, dark	
G	Warm, no water, light	
H	Warm, no water, dark	

b Where would you do the test on seeds B?

c How many seeds would you test in each set of conditions? Explain your answer.

2 A plant was kept under a bucket. After two weeks it looked like this:

It was then kept in the open field for the next month and watered regularly.

a Draw what the plant looks like now.

b What difference would you notice between the colour of the leaves before and after being taken out from under the bucket?

3 A farmer adds some fertiliser to his soil.

a Besides nutrients, what else must a plant take in to make new material and grow?

b In which part of a plant does it make its own "food for growth"?

c Which one of these statements is true?

A Plants eat soil which is turned into new plant material.

B Plants absorb water from the soil to help them grow.

C Plants only use soil to anchor themselves down.

5 Earth's movements

In this unit, I am learning:

- how the Earth, Moon and Sun move relative to each other
- why we have night-time and daytime
- why we have regular seasons every year
- about the life and discoveries of some famous space scientists.

Key words

Earth Moon
Sun

Have you ever thought about what causes day and night?
You probably know it is to do with the way the Earth moves.

The movement of the **Earth** and **Moon** are linked to how we measure our days, months and years.

The **Sun**, Earth and Moon.

1 **What do you already know about the Earth, Moon and Sun?**

Work in small groups.

In your Workbook, make a note of 'Things we are sure of' and 'Things we do not really know'.

Give your group's list to your teacher to check.

WB 79

5.1 The apparent movement of the Sun

In this section, I am learning:

- to track the path of the Sun across the sky
- to explore how shadows are affected by the position of the Sun
- to explore sunrise and sunset times.

Keywords

Earth, interpret, research, Sun, sunrise, sunset

Have you noticed how the shadow of a tree points in different directions at different times of day? Why do you think this happens?

Hint

Think about the positions of the tree's shadow, the size of the shadow, the **Earth** and the **Sun**.

1 Looking at shadows

Work in pairs.

a. Track the position and length of the shadow of a stationary object at your school for a whole school-day.

- To find your object, go outside your classroom on a sunny day and look for something that has a shadow. For example, you can choose a tall post, a stick or a waste bin.
- Use a piece of chalk or a camera to record the shadow's size, shape and position when the Sun is out.

b. What changes over the day?

c. What stays the same all day?

WB 80

Why do shadows change during the day?

At the start of the day, the Sun is low in the sky in the east. This makes the shadows very long. At dawn, the tree's shadow is much longer than the tree itself.

During the day, the Sun rises to its highest point in the south. This happens in the middle of the day and is called "midday" or "noon". This is when the shadow of the tree is shortest.

The Sun then moves across the sky towards the west. The tree's shadow gets longer and longer until the Sun sets. At this point, the Sun disappears below the horizon. It is no longer visible and night-time starts.

Shadows change during the day because the Sun's position in the sky changes.

When the Sun is high above the horizon the shadows are short. When the Sun is low in the sky the shadows are long.

Long and short shadows

This bar chart shows the length of the shadow of a tree in Beijing, China. It was measured every hour from sunrise to sunset on one day in March:

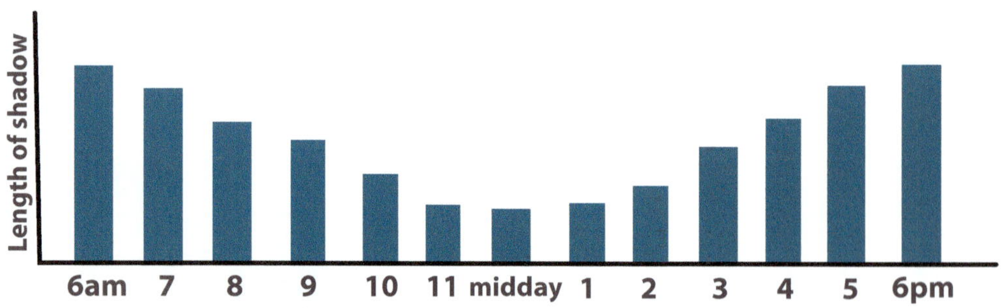

2 **Beijing data**

Look at the bar chart.

Interpret the data to answer these questions in your Workbook.

a. How many hours of daylight did the people in Beijing have on that day in March?

b. In Beijing, spring starts near the end of March. Summer starts in June.

What would the bar chart look like if the shadows were measured in June?

WB 80

Comparing sunrise and sunset data

The times of sunrise and sunset change each day. This depends on where you are in the world.

Look at the sunrise and sunset data for Mumbai, India, at different times of the year:

Date	Sun rises at ...	Sun sets at ...	Number of daylight hours
1st March	6.42	18.48	12.06
1st June	6.02	19.18	13.16
1st September	6.27	18.36	12.09
1st December	7.06	18.06	10.59

3 Sunrise and sunset in Mumbai

You can plot the sunrise and sunset data for Mumbai on a graph.

a. Plot the sunset data on the graph in your Workbook.

b. The vertical line shows how long a day is. Draw vertical lines between the two points for June, September and December.

- When was the longest day in Mumbai?
- When was the shortest day in Mumbai?

WB 81

In this section we looked at the **apparent** movement of the Sun in the sky. But the Sun does not actually move across the sky. The Earth spins, which gives the impression the Sun is moving.

You will learn about the rotation of the Earth in the next section.

Extension

Research the sunrise and sunset times where you live.

WB 82

Checklist

Complete the checklist on page 83 in your Workbook.

- I can track the path of the Sun across the sky.
- I understand how shadows are affected by the position of the Sun.
- I can explore sunrise and sunset times.

5.2 The spinning and orbiting Earth

In this section, I am learning:

- how to model the movement of the Earth and Sun to explain day and night
- that the Sun does not move around the Earth
- that the Sun appears to move because the Earth is spinning on its axis
- how to model the movement of the Earth and Sun to explain the length of a year
- that the Earth orbiting the Sun causes our different seasons.

Key words

24 hours	axis
day	Earth
Jupiter	Mars
Mercury	Neptu
night	orbit
research	Saturn
solar system	spin
Sun	Uranu
Venus	year

Modelling the Earth's movement

In section 5.1 you learned about how the **Sun** seems to move across the sky. For a long time, people believed that the Sun moved around the **Earth** to give us **night** and **day**. In fact this is an optical illusion.

The Earth **spins** constantly, but the Sun stays still. The spinning Earth makes it look like the Sun is moving.

Your teacher will show you a globe. The globe models the Earth. Notice it is tilted at an angle

Watch as the globe spins around. We say that the Earth is spinning around its own **axis**.

The model of the Earth has a metal rod, which the globe spins around. This models the axis.

The real planet Earth tilts at the same angle – but there is no rod running through the Earth!

Modelling planet Earth and its axis

Day and night

Look at the diagram.

The imaginary line drawn through the Earth in the diagram is its axis. It runs through the Earth from the North Pole to the South Pole. The Earth spins around this axis once every **24 hours**. As it spins, half of the surface of the Earth passes from sunlight into darkness. This is what gives us day and night in a 24-hour period.

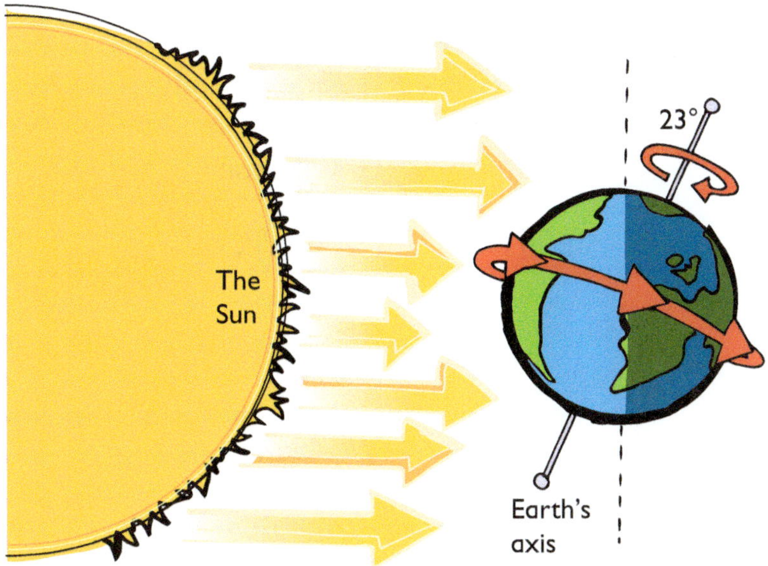

Sunlight reaching the Earth

Modelling day and night 1

In a dimly lit room, your teacher will use a globe (the Earth) and a torch or lamp (the Sun) to model how we get day and night.

Stick a modelling-clay figure on the globe where you live.

a. Turn the globe to show how the Earth moves when the figure is at:

- breakfast time
- lunch time
- bedtime.

b. Turn the globe so the country you are in is in daylight. Where on the Earth is it night-time?

c. How many hours does it take the real planet Earth to spin all the way round once?

WB 84

Model globes often show the tilted axis of the Earth. The light from a torch models sunlight.

Day lengths

The Earth is one of eight planets in the **solar system**. The other planets are: **Mercury**, **Venus**, **Mars**, **Jupiter**, **Saturn**, **Uranus** and **Neptune**. In Stage 7, you will learn that each planet has its own length of day.

The hours of daylight on Earth vary:

- at different times of the year
- in different places.

In summer, there are more daylight hours. In winter, there are fewer daylight hours. But this is not what we mean by the length of day on a planet.

Each planet spins around its axis at different speeds. The time it takes a planet to complete one whole turn is the length of its day.

It takes 24 hours for the Earth to spin round once on its axis. We call this time one Earth day.

2 Modelling day and night 2

Work in small groups.

a. Write a script for a parent to explain to a 6 year old child how we get night and day. Use a football or basketball to represent the Sun and a tennis ball to represent the Earth.

b. Take it in turns to act out the role of the parent.

WB 84

Extension

a. Why is it useful to model the Sun as a football and the Earth as a tennis ball?

b. Why is this also a poor model of the real Sun and Earth?

WB 84

Interesting fact

A day on the planet Mercury is almost 59 "Earth days" long.

The orbiting Earth

We have seen how the Earth constantly spins on its axis. It does one complete turn in 24 hours, causing night and day.

As the Earth spins, it also travels through space around the Sun. We say that the Earth **orbits** the Sun. The Earth orbits the Sun in an almost circular path.

The time it takes the Earth to complete one orbit of the Sun is called a **year**. During one complete orbit of the Sun, the Earth spins on its axis just over 365 times. That's why we have 365 days in a year.

Interesting fact

It actually takes 365¼ days for the Earth to orbit the Sun. You can't have a quarter day in a year. This is why we have 365 days for three years and every fourth year we have an extra day, 366 days. We call that year a 'leap year'.

Extension

Mercury spins very slowly. It takes 60 "Earth days" to spin once. Mercury takes 90 "Earth days" to complete an orbit around the Sun. So in one "Mercury year" there are only one and a half days.

Use a model to explain this to a partner, then write an explanation in your Workbook.

WB 85

3 Earth timings

Work in pairs.

- Who can answer these questions about time more quickly?
- You will both need a calculator.

Start your timer.

a. How many seconds are there in a minute?
b. How many minutes are there in an hour?
c. So how many seconds are there in an hour?
d. How many hours are there in a day?
e. How many days are there in most years?
f. How many hours are there in most years?
g. How many hours are there in a leap year?

Stop your timer.

h. Check your answers with each other – ask your teacher if necessary. Add 20 seconds to your time for each wrong answer. Who was faster?

After the timed test, write your answers in your Workbook.

WB 85

Seasons of the year

Look at the Earth orbiting the Sun, below.

The Earth spins about an imaginary line – the axis. This axis tilts at about 23 degrees as the Earth goes around the Sun. It always tilts in the same direction.

This tilt causes the part of the Earth that is north of the equator (called the northern hemisphere) to point more towards the Sun from May to August. During these months, the southern hemisphere points away from the Sun.

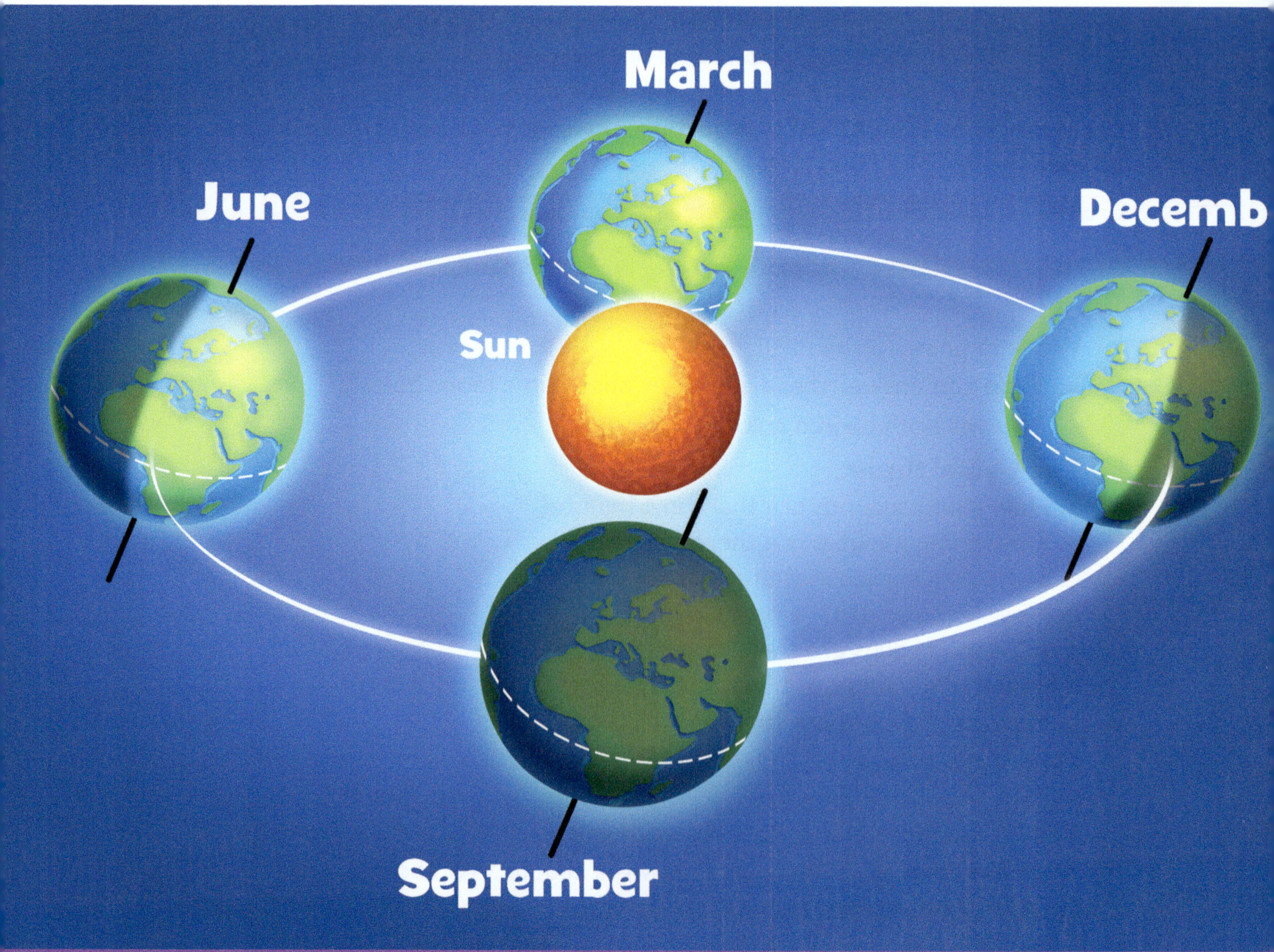

When the northern hemisphere points towards the sun from May to August:
it gets more sunlight

- it is warmer because of this extra sunlight
- daytime is longer.

This is the season of summer for places in the northern hemisphere.

When the southern hemisphere tilts away from the Sun in these months:

- daytime is shorter
- it is colder.

This is the season of winter for places south of the equator.

In the next six-month period, September to April, the opposite applies. The Earth moves to the other side of the Sun. Then the southern hemisphere has its summer and the northern hemisphere has its winter.

Interesting fact

If you live near the equator, the temperature is very similar all year round. Your seasons will be wet or dry, rather than hot or cold.

4 **Seasonal differences**

Work in pairs.

Discuss these questions and write your answers in your Workbook.

a. Do you live in the northern or southern hemisphere? In which months do your summer and winter take place?

b. What are the main differences in the weather between the seasons in your year?

c. Explain any differences in temperature using the diagram of the Earth and Sun on page 98.

d. Describe how one animal is affected by the different seasons where you live.

e. How can you tell when springtime is on its way?

WB 86

5 Modelling the orbiting Earth

Work in pairs.

a. Decide who will be the Earth and who will be the Sun.

b. How can you act out the movements of the Earth around the Sun?

The person acting as the Sun should give a description of what is happening, mentioning:

- day and night
- the seasons
- the length of a day
- the length of a year.

WB 87

Extension

Carry out research to find out which planet has the longest day and which planet has the shortest day.

WB 87

Checklist

Complete the checklist on page 87 in your Workbook.

- I can model the movement of the Earth and Sun to explain night and day.
- I know that the Sun does not move around the Earth.
- I know that the Sun appears to move because the Earth is spinning on its axis.
- I can model the movement of the Earth and Sun to explain the length of a year.
- I know that the Earth orbiting the Sun causes our different seasons.

5.3 Space science

In this section, I am learning:

- about the different approaches scientists (including space scientists) can take to answer their questions
- about the life and discoveries of a space scientist
- to do a crater investigation making predictions, charts and measurements.

Keywords

asteroids, comets, conclusion, discoveries, evaluate, evidence, factor, fair test, galaxies, meteors, Moon, observe, orbit, planets, predict, present, research, scientists, space probe, stars, variable

Space investigations

Scientists try to find the answers to questions about the natural world and beyond. This includes the Earth, Sun and **Moon**, as well as the millions of **stars** and **planets** in the Universe.

Before they find answers, they must ask questions. Scientists use knowledge and existing data, and some creative thinking, to form sensible questions to ask. In Activity 1, you will think of some of your own scientific exploration questions.

1 Questions about the Moon

Make up your own questions about the Moon using the words below. The first question has been done for you.

a. How long does it take for the Moon to **orbit** the Earth?

b. Where ...... ?

c. Why ...... ?

d What ...... ?

e. When ...... ?

f. Which ...... ?

g. Who .... ?

Interesting fact

The Moon orbits the Earth like the Earth orbits the Sun. It takes the Moon just over 28 days (called a lunar month) to orbit the Earth once.

WB 88

Finding the answers to scientific questions

Scientists use different ways to find the answers to their questions.

Here are some examples.

Example questions	How to find the answer
How many **comets** can be **observed** through a fixed telescope in an hour?	**Observing, exploring and recording**
How long does it take the planet Mars to orbit once around the Sun?	**Researching – using secondary sources**
What **factors** affect the size of craters on the Moon (using clay to model meteors, and sand to model the surface of the Moon)?	**Fair testing – controlling variables**
Is there a link between the size of planets and their number of moons?	**Pattern seeking – making links from data collected**
How can we explain "day and night"?	**Using models**
What type of star is this?	**Identifying and classifying**
How can we design a telescope to make images of objects in distant **galaxies** even more clear?	**Designing things to solve problems**

Interesting fact

We always see the same side of the Moon – we never see the far side. A Russian **space probe** called Luna 3 carried a camera that first photographed the far side of the Moon in 1959. This was the first time that the far side of the Moon had been seen.

2 Mix and match scientific questions

Work in pairs.

How would you approach these scientific questions?

Choose from the examples in bold in the table above and in your Workbook.

a. How does the length of a telescope affect how much it can magnify objects?

b. What is the temperature on the surface of the planet Jupiter?

c. How can you make your own telescope?

d. What type of star is our Sun?

e. Does the size of a planet affect the distance it is found from its sun?

f. Why do planets have different lengths of day?

g. What changes do you see when you record what happens to the shape of the Moon over a month?

Hint

Question **f** can be explained by using different-sized balls.

WB 89

Nowadays a lot of space science (called astronomy) is carried out by making observations of outer space using powerful telescopes. Any new observations or measurements are explained by applying knowledge and using creative thinking, including mathematics.

3 Researching a space scientist

Write a brief report on the life and **discoveries** of a famous space scientist (astronomer).

Use the second method from page 102 – research using the internet or reference books.

Here are some suggestions:

William Herschel, Clyde Tombaugh, Henrietta Leavitt, George Abell, Norman Lockyer, Jocelyn Bell Burnell, Edwin Hubble, Tycho Brahe.

WB 90

Hubble space telescope

The Hubble telescope was named in honour of astronomer Edwin Hubble.

Images taken by the Hubble telescope

Investigating the surface of the Moon

On a clear night you might see a full Moon. There are patches of darkness visible on the Moon. Many of these are craters (huge hollows) in the Moon's surface. The craters were caused by collisions with chunks of rock called **meteors**.

The surface of the Moon shows **evidence** of past collisions with meteors or even larger rocks called **asteroids**.

In Activity 4, you will investigate what factors might affect the size of craters on the Moon. You will use a tray of damp sand to model the surface of the Moon and modelling clay to represent the meteors that collide with it.

Before starting your investigation, consider how you will measure the size of the "craters" made in the sand. Will it be easier to:

- measure the depth of the falling ball of clay (the "meteor") in the sand (the "Moon" surface)
- measure the width (diameter) of the hole made (the "crater")?

How can you **improve the reliability** of the measurement?

If you repeat each test three (or more) times and take the average measurement, you can have more trust in your data.

If the three repeat measurements are similar, you can trust the average reading. If they differ and are really spread out, you probably need to do more tests. You can label any measurements that are obviously wrong and ignore them when taking the average.

Interesting fact

The Aitken basin is the largest crater on the Moon at about 2 500 km across and 6 km deep in places.

Before you begin your investigation, design a table to record your repeat readings and averages.

To do this, divide the second column of your two-column investigation table into four columns. For example, a scientist might investigate "How does the mass of the meteor affect the diameter of a crater?", so the headings in their table could be:

Mass of meteor in g	Diameter of crater in cm			
	1st try	2nd try	3rd try	Average

You are now ready to do your own investigation. How does the speed of the meteor affect the size of a crater?

4 Plan your crater investigation

Plan your investigation into the effect of the speed of a meteor on the size of the crater.

a. Make a **prediction**, explaining your reasoning.

b. What **variable** will you change in each test?

c. How you will get the meteor (clay ball) to drop at different speeds? Think about using a metre ruler. (The higher you drop the ball from, the faster it will hit the sand.)

d. What variable will you measure to judge the effect of changing the speed?

e. What variables will you need to keep the same in each test for fair testing?

f. Draw a table to record your results.

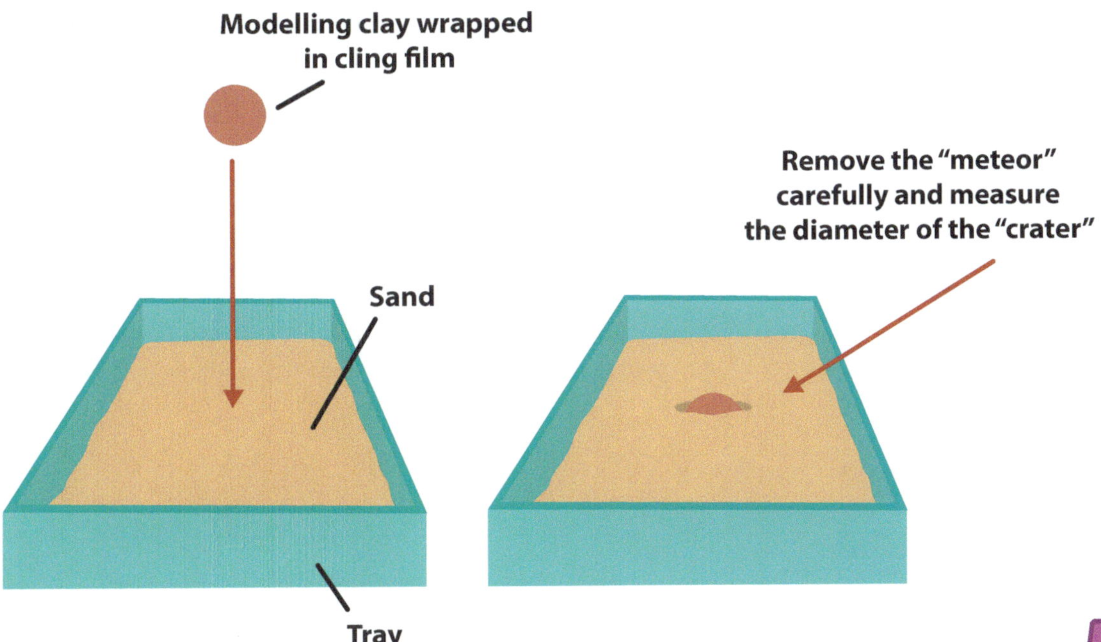

WB 91

5 Complete your crater investigation

a. Carry out your investigation and record the results in the table you drew in Activity 4.

b. Draw a graph to **present** your results – will you choose a line graph or a bar chart (see page 83)?

c. Do your results show a pattern? What is your **conclusion**?

d. **Evaluate** the quality of your repeat measurements.

- Were the three repeat measurements in each set grouped closely together?
- Are your results reliable?

WB 92

Checklist

Complete the checklist on page 92 in your Workbook.

- I know about the different approaches scientists (including space scientists) can take to answer questions.
- I have researched the life and discoveries of a space scientist.
- I have investigated the size of craters on the Moon and:
  – I understand the need for repeated measurements
  – I can present results in tables, bar charts and/or line graphs
  – I can decide whether results support predictions and evaluate repeated results.

What have I learnt?

Answer these questions on the worksheet your teacher gives you.

1 Which of these best describes the shape of the Sun?

A Crescent
B Circle
C Sphere
D Semi-circle

2 **a** Which four of the statements A–I are true?

A The Earth orbits the Sun.
B The Sun orbits the Earth.
C The Earth is bigger than the Sun.
D The Sun is bigger than the Earth.
E It takes the Earth 24 hours to spin around once.
F It takes the Earth 28 days to spin around once.
G It takes the Earth one year to spin around once.
H The Earth spins like this:

I The Earth spins like this:

b Explain how we get night and day on Earth.

3 **a** Draw a line on a copy of the picture below to show the path of the Sun across the sky.

Put arrows on your line to show which way the Sun appears to move.

b Draw a cross (x) on your picture to show when the shadow of the house will be shortest.

c Why does the Sun appear to move across the sky?

d Which two of these statements are true?

A The Sun rises earlier in winter than in summer.
B The Sun rises earlier in summer than in winter.
C The Sun rises at the same time all year round.
D The Sun sets earlier in winter than in summer.
E The Sun sets earlier in summer than in winter.
F The Sun sets at the same time all year round.

4 The diagram below is not drawn to scale:

a Draw a loop on a copy of the diagram above to show how the Sun and Earth move relative to each other.

b On the line you have drawn, write down how long it takes for one complete orbit.

c Which of these statements is true?

A We can see the whole surface of the Moon.
B We can only see one side of the Moon.

6 Shadows

In this unit, I am learning:

- about opaque materials, translucent materials and transparent materials
- that shadows are formed when light travelling from a source is blocked
- how the size of a shadow is affected by the position of the object
- to investigate how shadows change in length and position throughout the day
- how light intensity can be measured.

Key words

light
light intensity
opaque
shadow
translucent
transparent

Some cities are made up of blocks of buildings on grids of straight roads. At certain times of the year the Sun will rise or set exactly in line with a street to make stunning **shadows** and a **light** show.

1 What do you know about shadows?

Work in pairs.

a. Can you have a shadow in a totally dark room?

Discuss your ideas, then write your thoughts in your Workbook.

b. Make a pencil stick upwards on your table. You can use modelling clay to support the pencil.

Take turns to shine a torch at the pencil.

- Can you make the shadow longer or shorter? How can you do this?
- Can you make the shadow change direction? How can you do this?

WB 95

6.1 How do shadows form?

In this section, I am learning:

- that shadows are formed when light travelling from a source is blocked
- to observe and explain how shadows are formed
- to explain shadows using the idea of rays of light.

Keywords

block/blocked
design
evidence
light
light source
object
observe
shadow
silhouette
solid

1 Finding shadows

a. How many **shadows** can you see in this picture?

b. With a partner, look around your classroom. Find five more shadows.

c. Compare your shadows with another pair.

- What shadows did they find?
- Who found the biggest shadow?

WB 96

Exploring shadows

You will find out more about shadows as you explore them in the next two activities.

2 Making shadows

Work in pairs.

a. Use a hand torch to make a shadow. What shape is the shadow?

b. How many interesting shadows can you make? Can you make a shadow that looks like an animal?

WB 97

3 Design a shadow puppet show

Work in small groups to **design** a shadow puppet show.

a. You will need a piece of card, a pair of scissors, a thin stick and some sticky tape.

b. Draw a shape, perhaps a face or an animal or a person.

c. Cut around the shape.

d. Tape the card to a stick. This will form a **silhouette** on the wall or screen when it blocks out the rays of light from a torch.

e. Use a torch in a dark room to make your shadow puppet show.

What story can you create with your group? Put on a short show for others in your class.

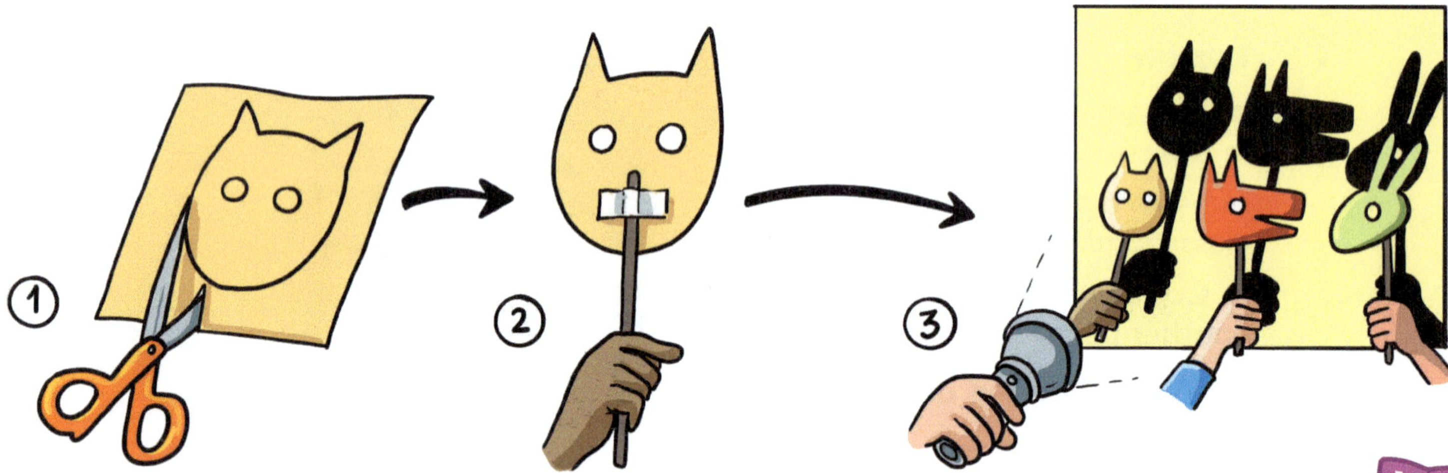

WB 97

Shadow formation

Now you have explored shadows, you will have **observed** that:

- there must be a **light source** to shine **light** on a **solid object** for it to have a shadow
- when an object **blocks** out the light rays hitting it, the area of darkness formed is the object's shadow
- shadows are found "behind" an object, opposite the light source
- the brighter the light hitting the object is, the darker the shadow appears
- a shadow is not always a sharp, black area with clear edges.

The formation of shadows provides **evidence** that light travels in straight lines (see Unit 1).

Using light rays to explain shadows

Light travels in straight lines, it does **not** bend. If rays of light could bend, objects would not have shadows. Why is this?

This diagram shows how a shadow is formed.

Look at the diagram. Does all the light from a torch come from a single point through the end? What effect might this have on the shadow formed?

Shadow of a book from a source of light

If light comes from a wide source, the shadow is divided into a darker part and a lighter outer part. The wider the light source, the more blurred the shadow. A torch is a non-point light source – light rays come out through the glass and end as a wide beam, not a single ray of light.

Extension

a. **In a darkened room, shine a hand torch on to a book with a wall or screen behind it.**

- **What do you notice about the shadow?**
- **Is a sharp, single shadow formed?**

b. **Explain your observations on a drawing in your Workbook.**

WB 98

4 **Explaining how shadows form**

As Amira was walking home at night, the streetlight made a shadow. Answer these questions in your Workbook.

a. Did Amira have a shadow when she stopped under the streetlight to cross the road?

b. How can Amira make her shadow much larger?

c. How are the shadows made?

Explain your answer in your own words. Use a drawing to help you.

WB 99

Checklist

Complete the checklist on page 99 in your Workbook.

- I know that shadows are formed when light travelling from a source is blocked.
- I can observe and explain how shadows are formed.
- I can explain shadows using the idea of rays of light.

6.2 Opaque, translucent and transparent materials

In this section, I am learning:

- the meaning of "opaque", "translucent" and "transparent"
- to investigate how to classify materials as opaque, translucent or transparent.

Key words
light
opaque
results
translucent
transparent

In section 5.3 we saw how classifying things is one of the methods we can use to answer scientific questions. Classifying means grouping things together based on similarities. Here we will look at classifying materials by exploring whether or not they can block light.

Grouping materials

Work in small groups.

Your teacher will give you different objects made from a range of materials. We are interested in the materials the objects are made from, not the objects themselves.

a. Sort the objects into groups based on the materials from which they are made.

b. Swap tables with another group. Can you guess how the other group has classified their materials?

Explain your reasoning for the groupings you chose to each other.

WB 100

Can you see how these objects have been classified into two groups?

Materials and light

When we shine a **light** on materials we find that they:

- let most light pass through
- let some light through
- let no light through.

Light travels through **transparent** materials.

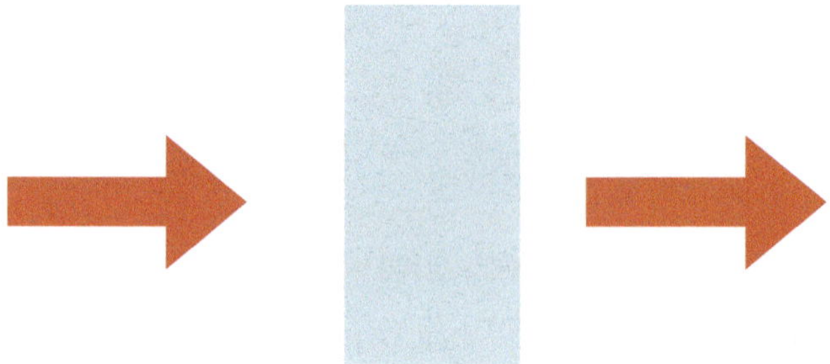

Some light travels through **translucent** materials.

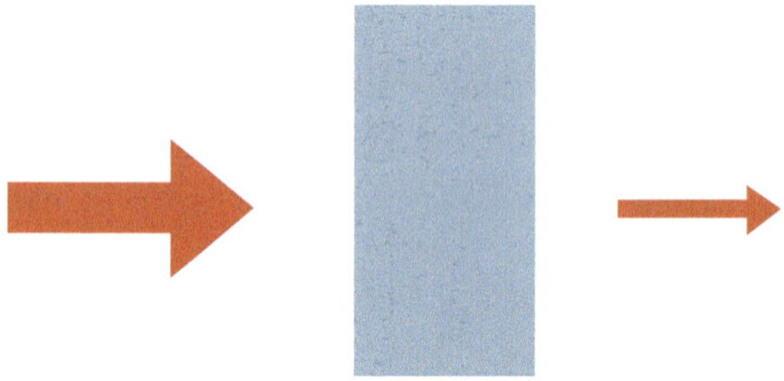

No light travels through **opaque** materials.

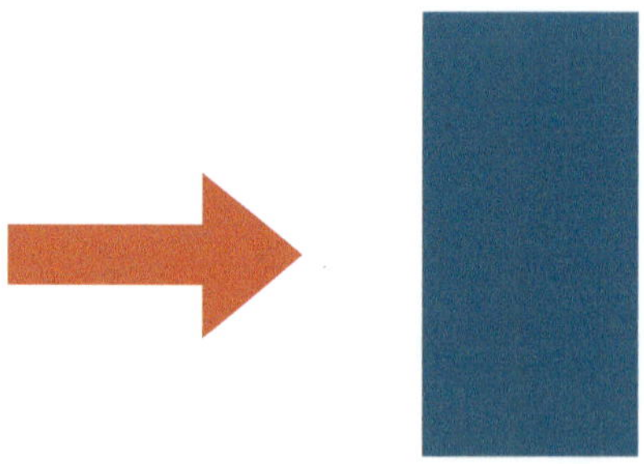

2 Making your own decisions

Work in small groups.

Your teacher will give you a torch and the same objects made from the same materials as in Activity 1.

Use the torch to test which materials are transparent, which are translucent and which are opaque.

Enter your **results** in the table in your Workbook.

WB 100

Uses of shadows

Shadows provide shade from the Sun. People have always made use of this. The buildings in this Mediterranean village were built hundreds of years ago. The streets are very narrow. The houses are often three storeys high. This provides as much shade as possible to keep cool in the hot summers.

Extension

The pictures show a toy boat and some shadow shapes. Which shape(s) can you not make using this boat and a torch?

WB 101

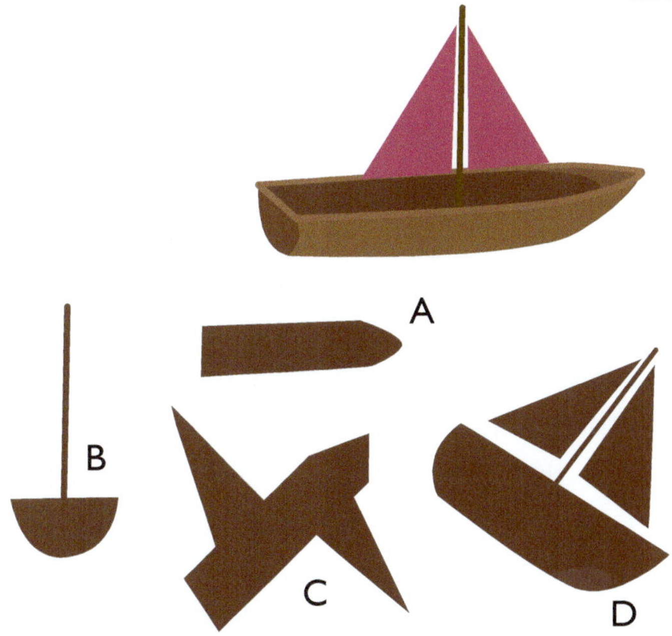

What else can people do to prevent bright sunlight coming into their homes?

Checklist

Complete the checklist on page 101 in your Workbook.

- I know the meaning of the terms opaque, translucent and transparent.
- I can investigate how to classify materials as opaque, translucent or transparent.

6.3 What affects the size of a shadow?

In this section, I am learning:

- to investigate how the size of a shadow is affected by the position of the object, including:
  - to make and explain predictions of what will happen
  - to plan how to carry out a fair test
  - to draw a graph of my results
  - to collect enough evidence to test my ideas.

Keywords

conclusion, factor, fair test, interpret, measure, measurements, object, observe, plan, position, predict, prediction, results, shadow, variable

Fair testing

You have explored lots of **shadows** – but you haven't done any **fair tests** on them yet. In section 5.3 you learnt that fair tests are another way of finding the answers to some scientific questions.

For example, your question might be: "How does the distance of an object from a screen affect the size of its shadow?"

In this example:

- the distance of the object from a screen is the **factor** or **variable** you choose to change in each test
- the size of the shadow is the factor or variable you **observe** or **measure** to judge the effect of changing the first variable.

Remember – in a fair test all the other variables should be kept the same in all your tests.

1 Listing variables

Work in pairs.

a. What variables can affect the size of an **object's** shadow? In your investigation the object is a pencil.

b. Why does Sook think that Bibek is joking?

c. Share your list of variables with another pair.

Agree on a final list of variables that might affect the size of the pencil's shadow.

WB 102

Each of the variables you listed in Activity 1 might affect the pencil's shadow. At this point you cannot be sure. You haven't tested anything yet!

Was one of your listed variables "**position** of the object"? In Activity 2 you can see how this affects the size of the pencil's shadow.

What question can you use to investigate the pencil's shadow? How will the variable you choose to change affect the variable you measure for each change made?

2 Planning and predicting

The question you will investigate is:

"How does the position of a pencil affect the size of its shadow?"

a. **Plan** your investigation. Look at the test below to help you.

- What will be the only variable you change in each test?
- How will you measure the size of the pencil's shadow? Look at the picture to help you.
- What variables will you keep the same in each test?

b. Make a **prediction** about how the height of the pencil's shadow will be affected by changing its position.

- Will you need to repeat your tests to make them more reliable?
- Is it easy to measure the height of the pencil's shadow? If not, why not?

WB 102

Trying out your shadow investigation

You are nearly ready to carry out your investigation and collect data to see if your prediction is correct.

You will need:

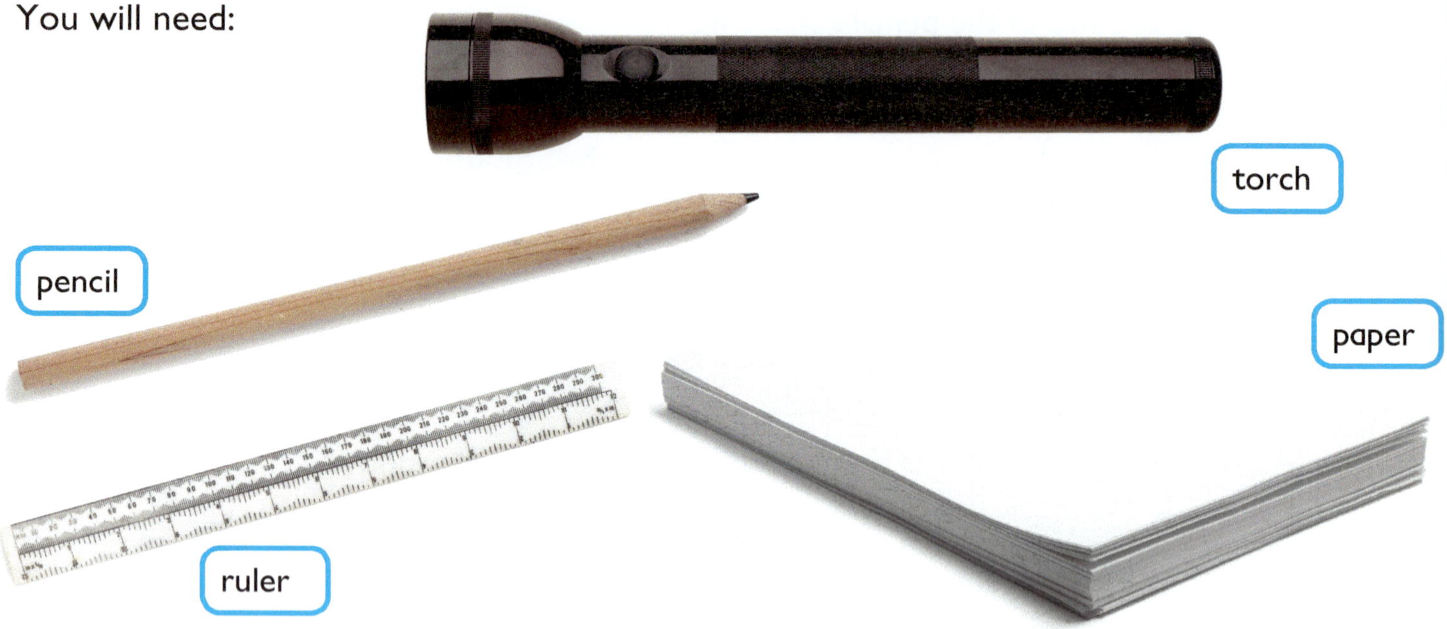

Before you start, you will need to do a trial run to see how far you can move the pencil and still get a shadow to measure on your screen.

Your screen can be a piece of paper or card, or a light-coloured wall. If you stick your paper or card to a wall, you can mark the heights of shadows on the screen. This makes measuring the height easier and more accurate.

3 Trial run

Explore where to place the torch and pencil so your shadows fit on the screen.

a. Find a good position for the torch.

b. Stand the pencil against the screen.

c. Turn the torch on and move the pencil slowly away from the screen.

d. Stop when the shadow is too big for the screen.

e. Measure the distance from the screen to the pencil.

WB 104

The measurement from your trial run gives you the range of positions to place the pencil in your tests.

You will draw a line graph of your **results** in Activity 5. You will need to measure the pencil's shadow in at least five different positions. The first position can be against the screen, at 0 mm. The last position tested will be the measurement you make in Activity 4.

Tables of results and carrying out your investigation

Now you can carry out your investigation. Use your work from Activities 2 and 3.

4 Carrying out your plan and recording

a. Draw a table to record your measurements. It may look like this:

Distance of pencil from the screen in mm	Height of pencil's shadow in mm
0	

If you plan to repeat your tests, divide the second column in the table to record each repeated test and the averages.

In your investigation, the table to record repeat measurements could look like this:

Distance of pencil from the screen in mm	Height of pencil's shadow in mm			
	1st try	2nd try	3rd try	Average
0				

b. Carry out your investigation and record your results in your Workbook.

- Make your **measurements** as carefully as possible. You can record them to the nearest millimetre.
- To work out the average of the three repeat results, add them up and divide by 3.
- For example, if three repeats were 155 mm, 151 mm, and 153 mm, you calculate the average like this:
  - Add up the three repeats: 155 + 151 + 153 = 459 mm
  - Divide by the number of repeats (3): 459 ÷ 3 = 153 mm

WB 104

Drawing a line graph

In Activity 5 you will draw a graph of your investigation results.

Whenever you draw a line graph:

- choose a sensible scale – your graph should take up most of the graph paper grid
- make sure your scale goes up in even amounts on each bold grid line – for example, 0, 1, 2, 3, 4 … or 0, 2, 4, 6, 8 … or 0, 5, 10, 15, 20 … or 0, 10, 20, 30, 40 … (do not go up in 3s as this makes the little squares difficult to judge)
- label both axes, including any units – for example 'Height of shadow in mm'
- plot your points as small 'x's using a pencil
- decide which variable goes up the side of the graph and which goes across the bottom (see page 83 to remind you).

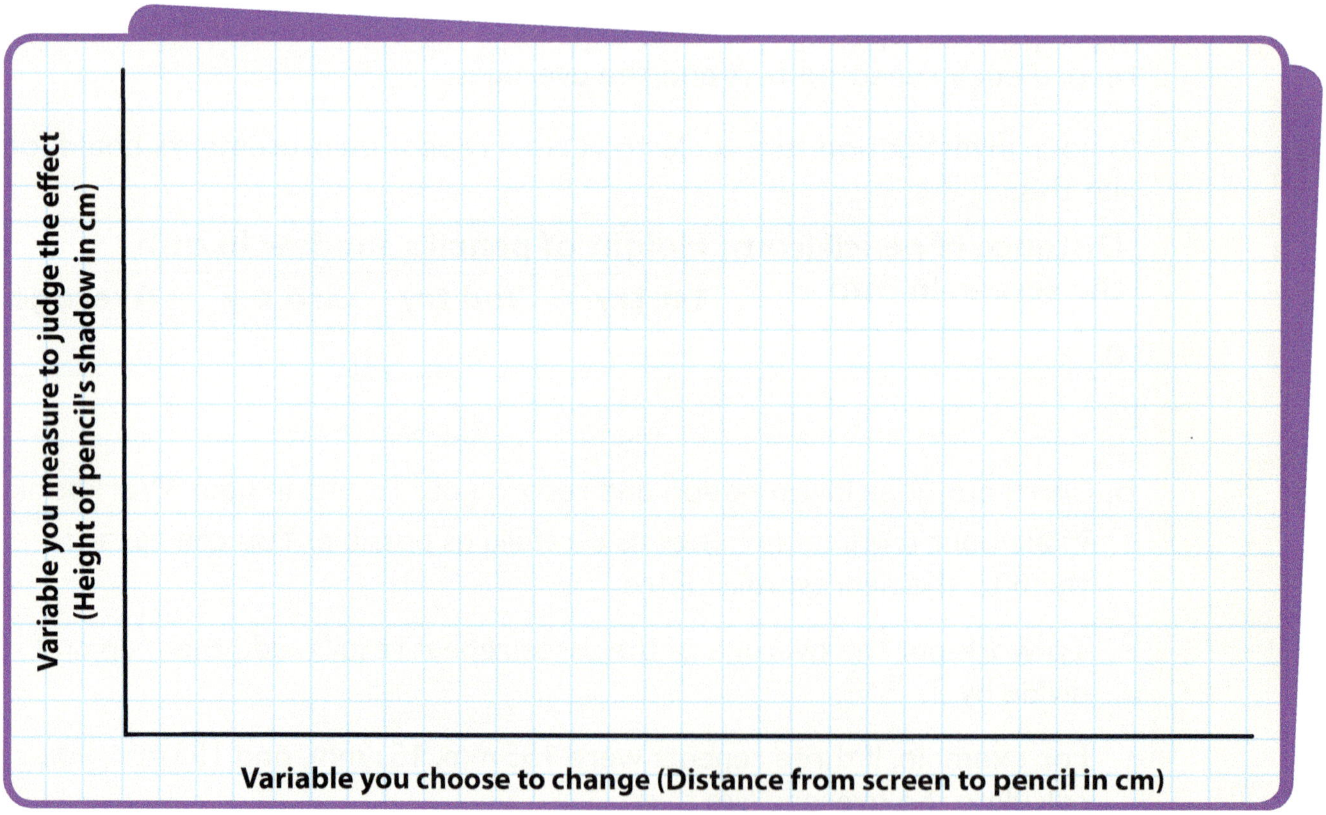

5 Presenting your results

Draw a line graph to show the results from your table in Activity 4.

You can see the labels for the axes in brackets on the graph grid above.

WB 105

6 Analysing your results

a. Look at your graph from Activity 5.

- What pattern can you see in your results?
- How do you **interpret** this pattern?
- Write your **conclusion** in your Workbook.

b. Does this agree with the prediction you made in Activity 2? Explain why.

WB 105

Evaluating your investigation

After your investigation, ask yourself "How can I improve my investigation?".

You might even think of some new questions about shadows.

Now finish the investigation by doing the evaluation exercise in the Extension box below.

Extension

Work in small groups.

Discuss the following questions to evaluate your investigation. Note your answers in your Workbook.

a. Did anything go wrong in your tests?

If it did, say what went wrong.

b. Was anything more difficult than you thought it would be? How can you change your plan to make it easier?

Explain how this makes your investigation better.

c. How can you improve your results? Did you take enough readings? Are your measurements accurate enough?

d. If you repeated your measurements and worked out the averages, did you find big differences in the sets of readings?

If so, explain why.

WB 106

Now you have finished your investigation. Is there anything else you want to find out about this topic?

6.4 The time of day and shadows

Keywords
length
observation
position
shadow

In this section, I am learning:

- how shadows change in length throughout the day
- how shadows change position throughout the day
- how we can use the Sun to tell the time
- how to make a sundial.

The girl on the scooter has a long shadow. Why is there a shadow?

In section 5.1 you looked at how **shadows** change at different times of the day. Remind yourself how the position of the Sun in the sky affects the shadows formed.

1 Sunny days, changing shadows

Work in pairs.

a. Go outside into the playground.

- Ask your partner to stand still in a sunny place.
- Draw around your partner's feet and their shadow with chalk.
- Write the time on the ground next to the shadow.

b. Go outside 30 minutes to an hour later.

- Ask your partner to stand in the same place.
- What has happened to the shadow? Write your **observations** in your Workbook.
- Draw around the new shadow and write the time.

c. Repeat this shadow task throughout the day.

- What patterns do you see in the **length** and **position** of the shadow outlines?
- Write these patterns in your Workbook.
- Share your findings with the rest of the class.

WB 107

Using the Sun to tell the time

In section 5.1, you learnt that the Sun appears to move across the sky because the Earth is spinning around all the time.

How long does it take for the Earth to spin around its axis once?

We can use the changing positions of shadows to tell the time. To do this, we use a sundial. Have you seen one before?

The shadow on the sundial shows the time.

2 Simple sun clock (sundial)

This sundial shows a time in the morning.

What time does it show?

WB 107

3 Making your own sundial

You will need:

- a piece of card
- a spiky cocktail stick
- a small piece of sticky tac or modelling clay.

You may need scissors to cut the card to make your dial.

a. Mark the hours on your sundial.

Morning hours are to the right.

b. Carefully push the cocktail stick through the centre. Fix it with a piece of sticky tac under the card.

c. Place the shadow stick so that, when the dial is sitting on a surface, the stick points **north**. (Use a compass to find north).

- The angle to set the stick depends on where you live. Some common angles are shown in the picture below.
- For your country, just push the stick to the best position to set the angle. It does not need to be too accurate.

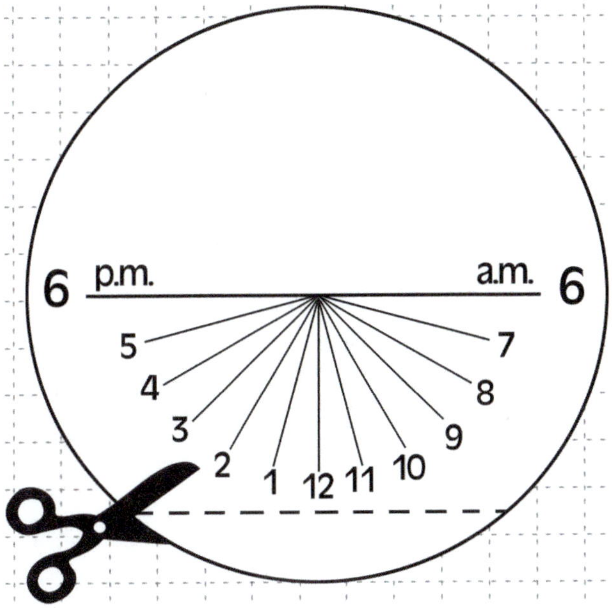

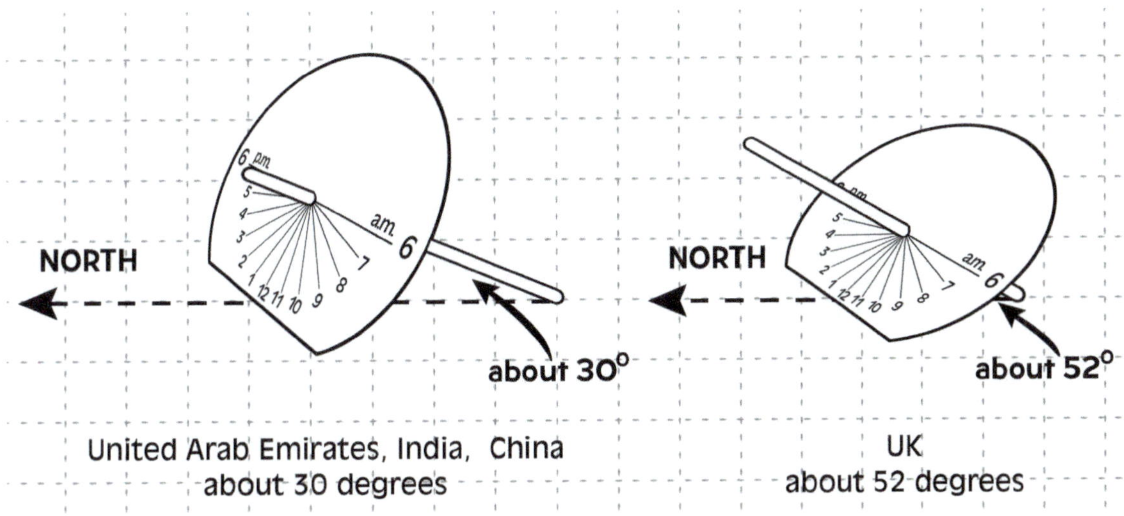

WB 108

4 How does a sundial work?

Work in pairs.

a. Discuss how a sundial works with your partner.

b. In your Workbook, explain how a sundial works in your own words.

Extension

Look at the shadow of the birdbath.
It is 10.30 in the morning.

a. Some other times are shown in your Workbook. Where would the shadows be at these times?

b. When can't we use a sundial to tell the time?

WB 109

Checklist

Complete the checklist on page 110 in your Workbook.

- I can investigate how the size of a shadow is affected by the position of the object, including:
  - I can make and explain predictions of what will happen
  - I can plan how to carry out a fair test
  - I can draw a graph of my results
  - I can collect enough evidence to test my ideas.
- I know how shadows change in length throughout the day.
- I know how shadows change position throughout the day.
- I can use the Sun to tell the time.
- I can make a sundial.

6.5 How bright is it?

In this section, I am learning:

- that the brightness of light in a place is called the light intensity
- that light intensity can be measured
- about where it is important to measure light intensity.

Keywords

fair test
light intensity
light source
measure
opaque
results
translucent
transparent

The intensity of light

In section 1.4 we saw how cricket umpires use light meters to **measure** how light it is. Batsmen are in danger if it is too dark to see the hard cricket ball thrown by a fast bowler.

The umpire's light meter reads the **intensity** (or strength) of the light.

1 Where else is light intensity important?

Work in groups of three.

a. At which other places or events is the intensity of light important? Explain why each answer is included in your list.

Think about:

sports reading photography farmers pilots astronomy

b. Share your list with another group. Then make and display a joint list for everyone to look at.

WB 111

Interesting fact

Astronomers need to gather as much light as possible from objects in outer space. Their telescopes use very large openings to capture enough light to see dim distant stars.

Data-logging and light intensity

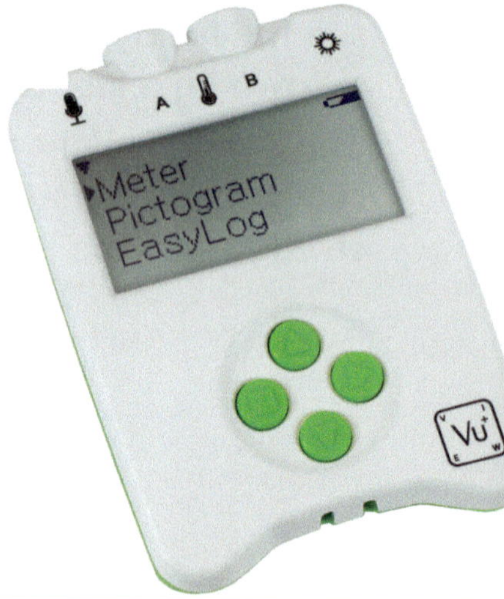

Scientists have developed very accurate light-measuring instruments. They can be linked to computers.

These data-logging light meters give readings and can monitor changes in the intensity of light over time. Look at the data-logger in the picture.

If your school has one or more light meters, investigate the following ideas.

2 How bright is a light bulb (or a candle)?

a. In a darkened room, use a light meter to find out how bright a bulb or a candle is at:

- 0.5 m away
- 1 m away
- 2 m away
- 3 m away
- 4 m away.

Before you start, sketch your predicted line on the graph axes in your Workbook.

b. Compare your predicted line with a line graph drawn using the data measured by the light meter. Or compare it to the graph displayed on the screen of a computer attached to the light meter.

WB 112

3 How bright is our room?

a. Measure the light intensity in your classroom with a light meter:

- with the lights on
- with the lights off.

b. With the lights on, where is the darkest shadow in the room?

c. With the lights on, is it brighter inside or outside?

WB 113

Translucency

In section 6.2 we saw how some materials are **transparent**, some are **opaque** and some are **translucent**. Tissue paper is a translucent material. It lets some light pass through it.

In Activity 4, you can use a light meter to investigate this property of tissue paper.

4 How much light gets through tissue paper?

Work in pairs.

Decide who will use a hand torch as a **light source** and who will use a light meter to measure the light intensity of the torch.

a. What is the light intensity at a distance of 20 cm?

b. What is the light intensity through a single piece of tissue paper with a light meter at 20 cm?

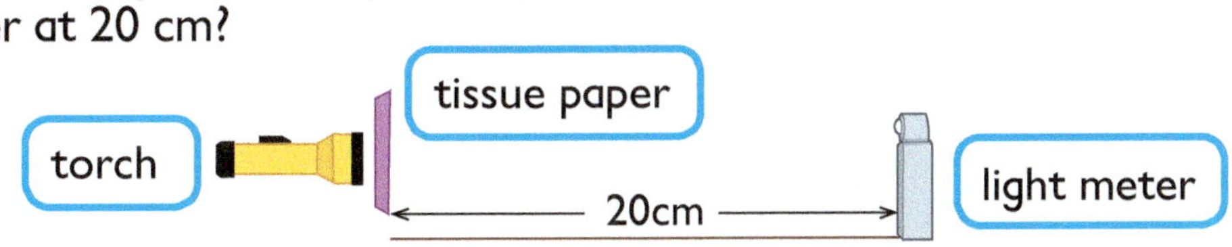

c. Predict how much light will pass through two pieces of tissue paper. How about three pieces?

d. Test up to five pieces of tissue paper and record your **results** in the table in your Workbook.

e. Check your predictions for two and three pieces of tissue paper.

- Were they accurate?
- How did you make this a **fair test**?

WB 113

Extension

a. Plot your results from Activity 4 on a line graph.

b. Use a ruler to draw a straight line through all the points plotted. Do not join them "x to x".

This "average" line is called a "line of best fit".

WB 115

Checklist

Complete the checklist on page 115 in your Workbook.

- I know that the brightness of light in a place is called the light intensity.
- I know that light intensity can be measured.
- I can describe some places where it is important to measure light intensity.

What have I learnt?

Answer these questions on the worksheet your teacher gives you.

1 Here is a sketch with some shadows.

a Some shadows are correct but others are wrong. Write down the letters of the wrong shadows.

b Look at the picture of a pencil and its shadow. Explain how this shadow was formed.

c Describe where you would move the pencil to make its shadow shorter.

2 **a** What do the following words mean?

i transparent **ii** translucent **iii** opaque

b Describe how you could test materials to find out if they are transparent, translucent or opaque.

3 A group were investigating shadows.
They set up the experiment below:

They changed the distance between the torch and the pencil.

a Describe how you could predict the position of the tip of the pencil's shadow on the screen.

Here are their results:

Distance between torch and pencil in cm	Height of shadow in cm
10	65
20	34
30	26
40	20
50	18

b Draw a graph to show these results.

c How does the height of the shadow depend on the distance between the torch and pencil?

Glossary

24 hours	The time it takes for the Earth to spin once on its axis. During this 24-hour period the Earth's surface passes from sunlight (day) into darkness (night).
apparatus	Materials or equipment used to carry out investigations or experiments.
asteroids	Rocky or metal objects that orbit (circle) the Sun. The size of an asteroid can range from tiny to five hundred miles across.
axis	The imaginary line through the Earth from the North Pole to the South Pole. The Earth rotates around this axis.
bar chart	A type of graph that uses horizontal or vertical bars to show the pattern of results.
beam	A broad path of light made by a non-point light source.
block/blocked	Something that gets in the way of (obstructs) the path of light, causing a shadow to form.
boiling point	The temperature at which a liquid boils. For example, the boiling point of water is 100 °C.
carpel	The female organ of a flower made up of the stigma, style and ovary. The stigma accepts pollen and the ovary contains eggs.
comets	Objects made up of dust, ice and gas that orbit the Sun and sometimes have a long, bright tail.
conclusion	A summary to explain what the results of an experiment or investigation mean.
condensation/ condense	The process of changing from a gas to a liquid. Condensation often happens when damp air meets a cold surface.
control	To manage something; to keep all variables in an experiment the same except for the factor under investigation (controlled experiment).
crystals	Minerals with a regular shape and a glassy appearance, for example, salt or sugar.
day	The time between sunrise and sunset. Can also mean 24 hours. This is the time it takes for the Earth to rotate once on its axis, passing from sunlight into darkness.
design	To make or draw detailed plans for something.
discoveries	Something that has been found out or learned.
discuss	To talk with another person or a group of people about something.

dispersal (wind, explosion, animal, water)	The movement or transport of seeds away from the parent plant. Seeds can be carried to other areas by the wind, by sticking to the fur of animals, by being eaten by animals and being excreted in their waste, by floating on water or by being projected by exploding fruit or pods.
Earth	The planet on which humans live.
energy	The ability to move or do work.
evaluate	To think about how well something has been done and consider ways in which it could be done better.
evaporation/ evaporate	To change from a liquid into a vapour (gas). Evaporation can happen below the boiling point of a liquid.
evidence	The available information that can be used to show or prove that something is true.
explain	To make clear in speech or writing; to make something understandable.
eyes	The organs with which people and animals see light and things; sight is one of the five senses.
factor	Something that has an influence on a situation or causes something to happen.
fair test	An experiment in which only one thing is investigated, keeping all other things the same.
fertilisation	The moment when a sperm and egg come together in animal fertilisation; the joining together of the male pollen and female ovum to create a seed.
filter funnel	A funnel used in a laboratory or science experiment to separate liquids from solids.
filter paper	A cone-shaped piece of paper used inside a filter funnel to act like a sieve. Filter paper has very tiny gaps between the fibres in the paper that separate small bits of insoluble solids from liquids.
flowers	The attractive, and often colourful, parts of a plant that attract insects and make seeds.
fruit	The part of a plant that grows from a flower and contains the seeds. Fruits contain vitamins and minerals and can be eaten as part of a healthy diet.
galaxies	Billions of stars held together by gravity. Earth and the Sun are in a galaxy called the Milky Way.
gas	A substance that spreads to fill the space, for example, air. Like most gases, air is invisible, but some gases are visible or have a strong smell, such as chlorine.
germinate/ germination	When a seed starts to grow into a new plant. Seeds need warmth, air and water to germinate.
growth	The process of increasing in size (growing).
image	A picture or photograph; a picture of something formed by a mirror, for example, a reflection.
insect	A small animal that has three parts to its body and six legs.
insoluble	A solid that does not dissolve in liquid, for example, sand in water.

interpret (findings) To understand or explain the meaning of the results of an investigation and reach a conclusion.

interpret data To understand or explain the meaning of the numerical results of an investigation and reach a conclusion.

investigate To look into or study something carefully and closely, possibly by carrying out experiments, to discover facts and information.

Jupiter The largest planet in the solar system.

length The distance from one end to the other; how long something is.

life cycle A series of changes or stages that a living thing goes through as it grows and develops. For example, a plant's life cycle is: seed > germination > young plant > adult plant > flower > fruit > seed.

light A form of energy that can be seen, for example, light from the Sun or a lamp; the opposite of shadow.

light intensity The strength or brightness of light in a place.

light source Something that gives out light.

line graph A type of graph that uses points connected by lines to show the pattern of results.

liquid A substance that pours and flows. A liquid fills the shape of a container. For example, water.

male Male animals fertilise female eggs; the male part of a flower fertilises the female part to make a seed.

Mars The seventh largest planet in the solar system. Mars is known as the red planet because of its colour.

measure Find the exact size, weight or amount of something by using a ruler, scale or other measuring device.

measurements The exact size or dimensions of something that is found by measuring.

melting point The temperature at which a solid turns into a liquid. For example, the melting point of ice is 0°C.

Mercury The second smallest planet in the solar system. Mercury is the closest planet to the Sun.

meteor A piece of rock from space burning up in the Earth's atmosphere. Also known as a shooting star.

mirror A sheet of glass with a coat of shiny metal on the back. The surface of a mirror shows a reflection.

Moon The large ball of cold rock that rotates around the Earth. The Moon reflects the Sun's light; it does not give off its own light.

Neptune The fourth largest planet in the solar system.

night	The time of darkness between sunset and sunrise when part of the Earth is facing away from the Sun.
object	Anything that has a shape or form and can be seen or touched.
observation	To make a comment or take notes on something that has been observed (watched or looked at).
observe	To look at carefully and notice what happens.
opaque	An object or material that does not allow light to pass through it.
orbit	The circular path that a planet follows when moving in space around another planet or star. For example, the Earth orbits the Sun.
ovum	The female reproductive part of a flowering plant.
particles	The tiny parts that make up all matter. Particles can only be seen with a special microscope. Models can be used to show how the particles inside a solid, liquid or gas are arranged and move.
petal	One of the separate leaves that form the outer part of a flower head. Petals are often colourful and scented to attract insects.
plan	To think ahead and develop or design an action. For example, an experiment, investigation or test.
planets	Large objects made of rock or gas that orbit the Sun. The eight planets in the solar system starting with the one nearest to the Sun are: Mercury, Venus, Earth, Mars, Jupiter, Saturn, Uranus and Neptune.
plant	A living thing that makes its own food using air, water and sunlight. For example, trees, bushes and grass.
pollen	The fine yellow powder made by a flowering plant. Pollen is made by the stamen (male part of the plant). When carried to another plant of the same species by the wind or an insect, it fertilises the ovum (female part) to make a seed.
pollination	The process of transferring pollen to the female parts of a flower.
position	The exact location of a person or thing.
predict/prediction	To think about and guess in advance what might happen based on observations.
present	To show or describe something.
present results	To show or describe your findings after carrying out an experiment.
ray	A very narrow beam of light shining in a straight line.
ray diagram	A simple diagram using arrows to show the direction in which a ray of light is travelling.
record	To write down or display findings.
reflect	To bounce back the image of something. For example, rays of light are reflected from the surface of a mirror.

reliable	To be trusted or relied upon.
repeat	To carry out or do something again.
reproduce/ reproduction	To have babies, to make seeds that grow, or to lay eggs that hatch.
research	To look up information about something.
results	Findings or information discovered through experimentation or investigation.
Saturn	The second largest planet in the solar system. Rings of ice circle around the middle of Saturn.
scientist	A person who works in science and whose job it is to find the answers to questions about the natural world and beyond.
seed production	The result of fertilisation when the ovum develops into a seed in the ovary of a plant.
seedling	A young plant that grows from a seed.
seed	The small part of a flowering plant that grows into a new plant.
sepal	A leaf-shaped part of a plant at the base of a flower head. Sepals hold and protect the petals in a flower bud.
shadow	The dark area created by a person or thing blocking the path of sunlight or other bright light.
show	To allow something to be seen or demonstrate something.
sieve	A piece of apparatus that has small holes and is used to separate solids and liquids or smaller solids from larger solids. For example, to sort beans into three sizes – small, medium and large.
silhouette	A strong, dark shadow cast on a wall, or a dark outline against a light background made by an object.
solar system	The Sun and all of its orbiting planets. The eight planets in the solar system (starting with the one nearest to the Sun) are: Mercury, Venus, Earth, Mars, Jupiter, Saturn, Uranus and Neptune.
solid	A material that has a fixed shape and does not flow.
soluble	A solid that dissolves in liquid, for example, sugar in water.
solution	A mixture of a liquid with a dissolved solid or gas.
spin	To rotate or turn. For example, the Earth spins on its axis.
stamen	The male part of a flower where pollen is made.
stars	Balls of glowing hydrogen gas that look like points of light in the night sky. There are millions of stars in the universe. The Sun is the closest star to Earth.
state of matter	Matter can be in three states: solid, liquid or gas.

Sun	The star in the centre of the solar system. The Sun is a large ball of burning gas that gives off heat and light. The Sun does not move.
sunrise	The time of day when the Sun rises in the East and can first be seen above the horizon.
sunset	The time of day when the Sun sets in the West and disappears below the horizon.
surface	The top layer of something.
test	To try something to find out information; a group of questions to find out how much someone knows.
translucent	A material that allows some light through but not all. Translucent materials are not completely see-through.
transparent	A material that is completely see-through. For example, clear glass.
Uranus	The third largest planet in the solar system.
variable	Something that can change; not constant.
Venus	The sixth largest planet in the solar system. Venus is surrounded by a dense, cloudy atmosphere that reflects light, making it the brightest planet.
warmth	The result of something being heated up.
water	The most common liquid on Earth and essential to life. Water is colourless, transparent, odourless and tasteless.
water cycle	The constant recycling of water in nature. Water moves from the sea to the atmosphere and back to the Earth or sea.
water vapour	Water in the form of gas; steam.
year	The time it takes the Earth to complete one orbit of the Sun. During this orbit the Earth spins 365 and a quarter times. Therefore, a year has 365 days.